BLOCK 6 PEOPLE IN GROUPS

UNIT 19/20/21

Prepared for the course team by Hedy Brown

SOCIAL SCIENCES: A THIRD LEVEL COURSE
SOCIAL PSYCHOLOGY: DEVELOPMENT, EXPERIENCE
AND BEHAVIOUR IN A SOCIAL WORLD

THE OPEN UNIVERSITY PRESS

Open University Course Team

Melanie Bayley *Editor*
Hedy Brown *Senior lecturer in social psychology*
Rudi Dallos *Staff tutor, Region 03*
David Graddol *Research Fellow, School of Education*
Judith Greene *Professor of psychology*
Jane Henry *Lecturer in educational technology*
Pam Higgins *Designer*
Clive Holloway *BBC producer*
Tom Hunter *Editor*
Mary John *Staff tutor, Region 02*
Maggie Lawson *Project control*
Dorothy Miell *Lecturer in psychology*
Eleanor Morris *BBC producer*
Stella Pilsworth *Liaison librarian*
Ortenz Rose *Secretary*
Roger J. Sapsford *Lecturer in research methods*
David Seligman *BBC executive producer*
Ingrid Slack *Course manager*
Richard Stevens *Senior lecturer in psychology*

Kerry Thomas *Lecturer in psychology, Course team chairperson*
Barbara Thompson *Staff tutor, Region 01*
Eleanor Thompson *Project control*
Pat Vasiliou *Secretary*
Doreen Warwick *Secretary*
Chris Wooldridge *Editor*

External Course Team Member
Jeannette Murphy *Polytechnic of North London*

Consultants
Charles Antaki *University of Lancaster*
Glynis M. Breakwell *University of Surrey*
Steve Duck *University of Lancaster*
Susan Gregory *University of Nottingham*
Patrick Humphreys *London School of Economics*
Kim Plunkett *University of Aarhus, Denmark*
Harry Proctor *Southwood Hospital, Bridgewater*

Course assessor
Professor Robert Farr *London School of Economics*

Set reading

S. D. Reicher (1984) 'St Paul's: a study in the limits of crowd behaviour', in the Course Reader (Murphy, John and Brown, 1984).

S. Milgram (1974) 'Problems of method', in the Course Reader.

'The perilous path: from social research to social intervention', chapter 2 of the Course Reader.

The Open University
Walton Hall, Milton Keynes
MK7 6AA

First published 1984. Reprinted 1988, 1991

Designed by the Graphic Design Group of the Open University.

Printed in the United Kingdom by Staples Printers St Albans Limited at The Priory Press.

ISBN 0 335 12228 0

This text forms part of an Open University course. The complete list of Blocks and Units in the course appears on the back cover.

For general availability of supporting material referred to in this text, please write to Open University Educational Enterprises Limited, 12 Cofferidge Close, Stony Stratford, Milton Keynes, MK11 1BY, the United Kingdom.

Further information on Open University courses may be obtained from the Admissions Office, The Open University, P.O. Box 48, Walton Hall, Milton Keynes, MK7 6AB.

BLOCK 6   INTRODUCTION

Why the study of groups is interesting

The study of people in groups has been a longstanding interest of social scientists and social philosophers and it has also captured the imagination and concern of ordinary people. The reasons for this are not hard to understand. First, and most important of all, the study of people in groups focuses explicitly on the extent to which individuals are independent of others and the extent to which they are influenced by them – an issue which is of concern to every individual and one which is also of scientific and political interest. (These issues were also raised in earlier parts of the course and the present Units will add to the understanding you have already gained.) Secondly, people spend a good deal of their time in association with others – at work, at home, and in leisure, political or religious contexts. It is not fortuitous that the first Units of this course took as their focus a universal group – the family. It is the family (whatever its form or range of functions) which first mediates the wider society's values and customs to the developing child.

We saw in Block 1 that not only is some form of family universal but that, as human beings, we are born with certain predispositions and attributes which stamp us as *social* beings: such attributes are essential to our survival since at birth and in infancy we are totally dependent on other people – even feral children must have had some human care at the start to survive. The new-born child's need for and innate capacity to respond to others form the initial basis for the process of socialization in the child's first social groups.

The 'need' for a response from other people may well be a life-long human trait and the basic reason why people spontaneously seek out others (even where there is no 'objective' reason for their being together as when a task needs their cooperation). As Cooley pointed out in 1902, small, spontaneously formed groups rather than single individuals may be thought of as the 'natural' basic human entity. It is the outcast, hermit and 'loner' who are deviants though they can survive, to some extent, outside human society since they already carry in their minds a symbolic representation of their social world which informs and constructs their behaviour and experience. They are also likely to have learned such skills as they need for survival before entering a state of isolation from others.

Levels of analysis

This course is subtitled 'development, experience and behaviour in a social world': the social world we focus on in the current Block is that of the group. It is

levels of analysis   usual among social scientists to identify three levels of analysis:

(a)   the individual;

(b)   the group; and

(c)   the larger society or culture.

These levels of analysis can be treated as distinct. However, for a full understanding of people and society we need to relate the theories and findings of each level to those of other levels since there are multidirectional influences between individuals, groups and society.

Individuals can adopt, reject or modify the wider society's values and standards and, as we shall see, group membership can be shown to be an important context and catalyst in which these psychological processes take place. In research on

dependent variable   groups most frequently the dependent variable (that is, that which is measured as the outcome) is the *group's effect on individuals* (in terms of modifications to

3

their perceptions, judgements, decisions, opinions or behaviour). However, the locus of explanation (the independent variable) can be conceived as being on a variety of levels of analysis and it is important to be clear in one's own mind as to the level at which one operates. Thus one can focus on factors which are attributes of *individuals*: their attitudes, values, personality traits; the 'fit' of their attitudes with those of others in the group; their need for acceptance by other people, in general, or by members of a particular group. All these may affect how people perceive group expectations or pressures and how they respond to them.

independent variable

individual level of analysis

Researchers and theorists can also operate at the level of analysis of the *group*, taking the properties of the group as their independent variables. Thus social psychologists have studied the social structure of groups, such as the pattern of communication which has sprung up informally among members or which has been imposed by the organizational structure of a firm or by the experimenter in the laboratory. The explanations on this level of analysis are no longer in terms of the attributes of the individuals comprising the group but in terms of the characteristics of the group which give rise to social interactions (which, it is assumed, would be of a different kind if the characteristics of the group were different). These, in turn, affect the individual members of the group.

group level of analysis

There is a further level of analysis, the *societal* level, which needs to be considered. Social interactions occur among individuals whose relative status, authority or power neither derive (wholly) from their own characteristics nor (wholly) from their position or roles in the group but (partly, though again not wholly) from the social context *beyond* the immediate group which is being studied. Thus, for instance, a teacher's influence may be determined not only by her or his personality, knowledge, teaching style and the match or mismatch between those attributes and the children's expectations, but by the status, authority or power inherent in a teacher's *role* as defined within the wider social structure. The attributes of such roles derive from the attitudes, values or ideologies prevalent in a given society. To account fully for the teacher's influence (or lack of it), we will therefore also need to study the teacher-pupils group from a *societal, cultural* and, indeed, *historical perspective* (since attitudes to authority may change over a period of time or be different in different societies). Explanations on this level of analysis are in terms of the social positions or social categorizations of the individuals involved. These explanations refer to factors beyond the immediate group though the evidence for their relevance and influence within the group will have to be noted in the changes they bring about (or to which they contribute) in individuals. Much of the research on groups has focused on intra-individual or intra-group factors and has neglected this societal level of analysis. It is, however, specifically considered when the interaction *between* groups is studied.

societal level of analysis

The notion of levels of analysis is important not only in research strategies and in the identification of the underlying causes of an event, behaviour or experience, but in terms of the search for remedies or improvements to a problem. Thus, for example, if we wish to change people's attitudes to and perceptions of racial minorities or the unemployed, we need to consider whether it would be more appropriate to effect change *directly* through persuasion and other psychological means (whether individually or in groups) or *indirectly* through changing the social context, for instance, by legislation; alternatively we may try to initiate change on all these levels.

Paper 3 in Part III of the Metablock discusses levels of analysis.

What is meant by the concept of 'group'?

The study of groups can thus be conducted at different levels of analysis and gives rise to many different questions. As we shall see (and have seen throughout the course) the precise questions which social psychologists have posed stem from

group their different theoretical orientations and from their awareness of contemporary social issues. Furthermore, the term group can be applied to many different entities – small or large groups, informal or formal groups, groups which have a short-term life (for instance, in a laboratory) and groups which have a more permanent existence. Groups also differ in their functions, purposes and goals, in their history and in the social context in which they occur. In these circumstances, it is inevitable that many different definitions of the concept of group coexist. I will not provide such definitions here, at the outset, but will discuss them in relation to the empirical or theoretical traditions which have given rise to them.

Indeed, a basic definition of a group, such as 'Two or more persons who are interacting with one another in such a manner that each influences and is influenced by each other person' (Shaw, 1971, p. 396) does not mean very much on its own and it prejudges the questions I have raised and which we will need to explore in order to arrive at answers and definitions. Shaw's definition may even confuse and annoy you at this stage as you might justifiably feel that a great deal of your course so far has already concerned itself with precisely such interactions without mentioning the term group. This raises the question of how useful the concept of the group is in explaining behaviour and subjective experience. Are we, in considering groups as a separate analytical entity, merely duplicating efforts at understanding made earlier in this course through other concepts or approaches, such as the notion of social exchange or the study of interpersonal attraction which you have explored in Block 3? Do these (chronologically) more recent approaches supercede the study of groups? Or do different approaches represent somewhat arbitrary research strategies which testify to the fragmented nature of social psychological knowledge? And is this why there are so few well-developed, wide-ranging theories in social psychology? We will come back to these questions at the end of the Block when *you* should be in a better position to arrive at an informed judgement.

Foci of research on the group

One interesting aspect of the study of people in groups is to follow the changing foci of research in this field as they develop from two interlaced strands:

(a)   the influence of the wider social context and what appears as 'problematic' in society (and hence the selection of *topics* or *issues* for research); and

(b)   developments and progress within the discipline (and hence *how* phenomena are studied and explained).

These two traditions of research – 'applied' and 'pure' – also broadly reflect differences in methodology. Thus the applied social psychologist tends to engage in field research and the pure theoretician of group processes, concerned not with social issues but with the advance of science, tends to use laboratory experiments. However, you will find that these distinctions have become somewhat blurred, certainly in the study of groups, and that many important issues have been researched by both the theoretician and the applied researcher, through field experiments and observation as well as through laboratory-based experiments. Equally, the applied researcher can hope to contribute to theory and the pure researcher may be able to extend our understanding of the processes at work in a 'real-life' issue. Indeed, one and the same person can take a problem into the laboratory and, at another time, study it in a more realistic context.

In this Block we will see examples of pure and applied research using a range of methodologies. We shall also see that research in this area raises ethical issues, concerning not only research methodology but also the use and implementation of research findings.

References

COOLEY, C. H. (1902) *Human Nature and the Social Order* (New York, Shocken, 1964).

SHAW, M. E. (1971) *Group Dynamics: The Psychology of Small Group Behaviour*, New York, McGraw-Hill.

UNIT 19/20/21
PEOPLE IN GROUPS

Prepared for the course team
by Hedy Brown

CONTENTS

Objectives

After studying this Block you should be able to:

1 Discuss the process of norm formation in small groups.

2 Distinguish between primary, secondary, membership and reference groups.

3 Understand the concept of group pressure.

4 Understand the concept of conformity.

5 Discuss the implications of Milgram's work on obedience to authority.

6 Outline the process of majority and minority influence in groups.

7 Describe some of the variables which affect leadership style and its outcomes.

8 Describe the factors affecting the impact of total institutions on individuals using Goffman's work and studies of political indoctrination and cults as illustrations.

9 Outline the social psychology of crowd behaviour.

10 Understand the concepts ingroup and outgroup.

11 Understand the concepts minimal group, personal identity and social identity.

12 Outline the work on bystander apathy.

13 Discuss the ethical issues of research in this field and of implementing research findings.

14 Discuss the appropriateness of different research methodologies in the contexts in which they have been applied.

Study guide

This Block spans three working weeks in your course and contains Units 19, 20 and 21. However, I have not divided the Block into Units as the material cannot easily be divided into three Units of approximately equal length. As you can see from the table of contents, you are presented with five sections.

In section 1 of this Block we will focus on the ways in which groups have been studied, both in the laboratory and in 'real' life. You may wish to spend the first week working through this section.

In section 2 we will explore the role of group membership in social control. We shall see that the insights gained from the study of groups give rise to the possibility that one may use group membership to change people, whether such a process is initiated by the members themselves, as, for instance, with a group of weightwatchers, or whether the initiative comes from outside the group, such as efforts at 'brainwashing'. This section may occupy you for your second week.

We will then move in section 3 to intergroup relations and the difficult question of whether and in what ways we should distinguish *interpersonal* relationships and behaviour (which you have studied in Block 3) from *intergroup* relations and behaviour. Here we will explore such topics as stereotyping, prejudice, intergroup conflicts and their possible resolutions, and bystander apathy.

In section 4 we will focus on crowd behaviour, a topic which was considered quite early in the history of social science (Tarde, 1890; Le Bon, 1895) and in which interest has re-emerged in the wake of recent events such as urban unrest, riots, vandalism and football hooliganism.

Finally, in section 5 we will explore the conclusions we can draw from the research we have discussed and their implications for social psychology. The study of sections 3, 4 and 5 is likely to occupy your third week.

As you proceed through the Block, you should reflect on three questions:

1   Does the Block put you in a better position to understand your own interactions in groups, for instance your relations with people at work, in a study group, or in the setting of the family?

2   Does it help you to make sense of the world around you and to understand phenomena which at first sight may seem incomprehensible? To take some specific examples, does the study of groups enable you to understand why Patti Hearst became an urban guerrilla in 1974 and maintained that role for a period of two years? Or how it came about that more than nine hundred people engaged in mass suicide in Guyana in 1978?

3   Is the concept of the 'group' (and the research and theorizing to which it has given rise) still a meaningful level of analysis in social psychology?

Set and recommended reading

The following articles in the Course Reader are set reading for this Block:

S. Milgram (1974) 'Problems of method'.

'The perilous path: from social research to social intervention', chapter 2 of the Course Reader.

S. D. Reicher (1984) 'St. Paul's: a study in the limits of crowd behaviour'.

The following recommended readings are also in the Course Reader and you will be directed to them at appropriate points in the Block:

B. Ehrenreich and D. English (1979) 'For her own good: 150 years of expert advice to women'.

H. B. Savin (1973) 'Professors and psychological researchers: conflicting values and conflicting roles'.

P. G. Zimbardo (1973) 'On the ethics of intervention in human psychological research with special reference to the Stanford Prison Experiment'.

P. Watson (1980) 'Captivity'.

The Metablock also meshes with this present Block. I would advise you to read (or re-read) the papers in Part III of the Metablock which are mentioned in the Block text.

You can read this Block as a whole and then turn to these articles in the Reader and Metablock or, if you prefer it, you can read them when they are referred to in the text.

The text is interspersed with some 'activities' to set you thinking and perhaps arguing with fellow students. These activities are not SAQs, that is, they do not have definite answers. So do not be discouraged if not all of them stimulate you to think about the issues to which they relate.

At the end of the Block you will find a list of further reading. These books and articles do not form part of your work for this Block but are suggestions if there are particular topics you wish to read more about.

1 GROUP MEMBERSHIP AND SOCIAL INFLUENCE: FROM CONFORMITY TO INNOVATION

Early empirical social psychology largely originated in the United States. From the 1920s American social psychologists explored substantive and significant problems in their society – race relations, urban problems, frustration and aggression, the development and change of opinions and attitudes, the relations of the individual to the group, the formation of social norms and issues relating to conformity. What strikes one in looking at this early work – and some of these studies remain fundamental to social psychology – is the underlying optimistic belief that knowledge can lead to progress and that scientific research will provide the basis for eradicating social evils. Even when these social psychologists carried out laboratory experiments they did so with the intention of testing important hypotheses about the *real world* and applying their findings to the description and explanation of behaviour found in actual social life. You may think that this is stating the obvious, but a good deal of social psychology today does not have quite this flavour: current work is more often concerned with the minutiae of behaviour rather than important 'macro' aspects of social life. As we shall see, like most American psychologists since Watson these early social psychologists were geared to looking for the causes of behaviour in the social environment rather than in the individual. As Cartwright (1979) wrote, 'McDougall's theory of instincts [that is, his notion that many quite complex behaviours are innate rather than learned] never really had a chance, not so much because it was wrong, which it may very well have been, but because it was antithetical to American culture'. Because of the importance and continuing relevance of these early studies, I will open our discussion by reference to some of these 'benchmarks' in social psychology.

1.1 The formation of social norms

As has been argued in earlier parts of the course, social life would not be possible unless people could reasonably predict other people's reactions to their own actions and they, in turn, were willing to modify both their actions and their expectations of the reactions of other people. In other words, our social relations
norms are governed by implicit and explicit norms which we see exemplified around us and which we tend to learn, both from experience and explicit teaching, and to which we spontaneously and routinely conform. The formation and change of such norms in the context of small groups – whether such groups had come together spontaneously or were set up in the laboratory – has been a focus of research since the 1930s. What preoccupied these researchers was their concern with the apparent tendency of people to adopt the views expressed by others and, therefore, the ease with which European dictators of that period had gained ascendency over public opinion and behaviour. These researchers attempted to
conformity unravel the nature of such conformity and to analyse the context in which it is likely to occur. We shall follow their explorations and will see that conformity is a complex phenomenon, not easily defined or distinguished from the effects of other social influence processes. We will discuss these ramifications after reviewing a number of influential studies.

I want to start our exploration of small groups with the study of the formation of social norms which was undertaken by Sherif (1936). His series of experiments reveals some important psychological aspects of the formation of norms and the effects of group membership on individuals. In these experiments Sherif was not concerned with the formation and adoption of social norms over a period of time, as would occur in primary or secondary socialization (discussed in Unit 4), but anomie

with the question of how an individual (or a number of people together) will react in a novel situation where she or he cannot fall back on previous experience, values or frames of reference and hence is afflicted by a sense of 'anomie' (that is, a lack of appropriate norms). What, then, did Sherif do?

Box 1 The formation of norms (Sherif, 1936)

autokinetic effect

Sherif seated his male subjects, initially one at a time, in a completely dark room in which the experimenter exposed a point of light for a few seconds. This point of light *remains stationary but appears to move*. This is an optical illusion known as the 'autokinetic effect'. The subjects were asked to estimate how far the light had moved in each of one hundred exposures. Wide variations were found in the judgements made by different individuals but each subjectively established a distinct range of estimates, peculiar to himself, and a characteristic personal 'norm' (the figure he called out most frequently), the result of basing later estimates on those made earlier. In other words, he established for himself a frame of reference in a situation where he lacked objective criteria because he found himself in literal and figurative darkness. When each individual was put into the same experimental situation again on subsequent days it was found that each tended to preserve his newly developed personal 'response norm' but made his estimates within a narrower range.

response norm

Sherif next turned to explore the reactions of individuals in two- or three-person groups. Would individuals again evolve their idiosyncratic frames of reference or would they act together in establishing a range, and a reference point within that range, peculiar to the *group*?

Sherif used two types of group situations. He studied the reactions of individuals who were put into the group situation first and only subsequently experienced the stimulus situation on their own. The reactions of these subjects were compared to those who first faced the stimulus situation alone and subsequently went through the experiment in groups of two or three. In all these situations, the subjects were instructed to give their *own* judgements and the post-experimental interviews confirm that they did not think of themselves as members of a group in which they would jointly arrive at agreed judgements. Nevertheless, whilst merely making their estimates in each other's presence what can only be called a 'group norm' emerged – quickly when subjects had not previously experienced this situation and a little more slowly when subjects had previously evolved individual ranges and norms (see Figures 1a and 1b). When individuals who had first experienced the situation together with other subjects subsequently faced the same situation alone they perceived it in terms of the range and norms they brought to it from the group situation.

group norm

What are we to make of Sherif's findings and do they help us in understanding the world around us?

First, these results demonstrate that the subjects in these experiments tend to structure unstructured situations: they establish for themselves a frame of reference within which they act with some confidence, in other words, *they impose a structure on a meaningless situation* and thus imbue it with meaning (a point extensively discussed in Block 4).

Secondly, these results demonstrate that subjects do not passively record what is going on around them but that the frames of reference which they develop in a situation, or which they bring to it, *modify the perception* of the stimuli to which they are exposed.

Figure 1a   Median estimates of movement in groups of two subjects

Figure 1b   Median estimates of movement in groups of three subjects

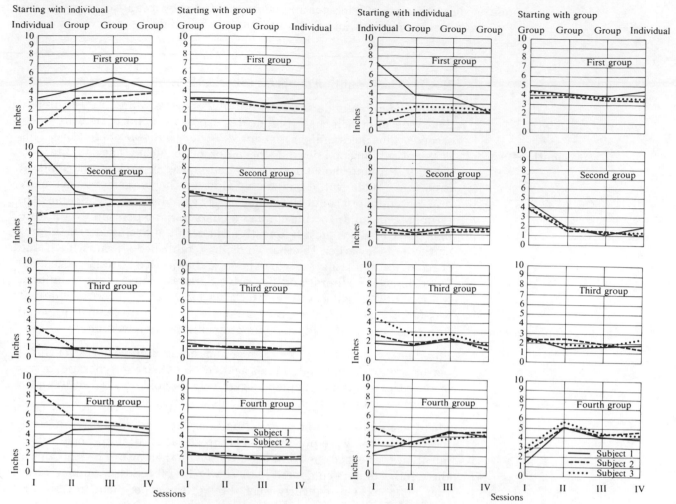

The graphs on the left in Figures 1a and 1b illustrate formation of group norms, where the individual has first evolved his own norms in estimating the distance the light moves.

The graphs on the right in Figures 1a and 1b illustrate that group norms are retained when the individual estimates distances on his own.

Source: Sherif, 1936

Thirdly, and this is what we are concerned with here, these results suggest that subjects *adjust their judgements to bring them into line with those of other people* even when they do not think of themselves as engaged in a common endeavour. We may infer that, at any rate in our culture, to be in accord with other people satisfies an important psychological need, particularly in situations where people lack certainty or the possibility of validating their own opinions other than by a comparison with those held by others. Through such 'social comparison' processes (discussed in Block 3) a common social reality is established and validated.

social comparison processes

social reality

Whilst Sherif's experiments (and later replications) almost invariably demonstrate this *convergence* of estimates among subjects in two- or three-person groups, post-experimental interviews reveal that the subjects themselves are unaware of being influenced, indeed hotly deny being affected by the estimates made by others in the group. It is interesting to speculate whether such subjects would have managed to evolve their own norms and range of estimates (and stick to them) if they had been told that a prize would go to the individual who made the 'best' estimates. We do not know since such an experiment is not recorded, but, given that the subjects were unaware of being influenced by others during these sessions, one might expect that they could not guard against such influences, whatever their motivation.

14

Sherif and Sherif (1969) report a study using the autokinetic effect which took place in a monastery. Here, apparently, conflict ensued between the monks and novices who were subjects in the same session and *convergence of estimates did not take place*. This study (though such explanations were not used at the time) may well illustrate the point I made in the Block Introduction concerning the need to take societal factors into account. Though one would expect the novices to agree with the monks (if only so as not to fall prey to the sin of pride) the tensions between them, or perhaps their perceptions of differences in their roles and status, 'intruded' into the experimental situation, even though it was an artificial situation which depended upon an optical illusion and was apparently divorced from any real-life event or concern.

In designing an experiment the experimenter assumes that her or his manipulation of the independent variable will determine the outcome. This is the essence of an experiment. Nevertheless we shall see further examples in this Block of 'intrusions' from outside the experimental situation, for instance from individual differences in the subjects which may affect the extent to which the independent variable has an effect. There are other difficulties in laboratory experiments, or rather in the interpretation of the findings. Thus in laboratory experiments subjects may not simply be affected by the experimenter's manipulations but may adopt a common identity or status as *subjects* which affects how they respond to the experimenter's expectations, as they, rightly or wrongly, perceive them.

Sherif's experiments are important because they are not simply applicable to the perception of an optical illusion: they mirror what we can see going on all around us, namely, that the expectations, attitudes and values of people influence their perception of and reaction to stimuli in their environment. Think, for instance, of your work situation. Could you understand your reaction to a change in work schedules, method of payment, the leadership style of the supervisor or anything else without reference both to your own previous experience and to the values, attitudes and expectations of the people around you? And these, in turn, will have resulted from *their* experience as members of the present work group and/or of other groups such as their union, family, social class and so on.

primary group

Sherif's work focused on a small group. Outside the laboratory such groups have often been referred to as primary groups because of their importance to the individual. Primary groups are always small groups in which all members have face-to-face contact. The relationships of people in such groups are therefore close and often intimate. Families, play groups, work or sport teams are examples of such groupings.

informal primary group

formal primary group

Small primary groups can be *informal*, that is, they can arise spontaneously, such as when children living in the same street congregate and form a gang. Primary groups, however, can also be *formal*, such as a work team brought together by management to accomplish a given task. In formal groups some of the important goals and roles of members are predetermined: for instance the expected standards of production, adherence to safety rules or behaviour towards colleagues are already laid down when a newcomer joins the firm. In informal groupings, on the other hand, goals, roles, attitudes and norms of behaviour tend to arise out of the current interactions of the group members. However, once established, adherence to such norms by individuals may indicate to others that they consider themselves, and wish to be considered by others, members of this group. The extent to which members uphold the group's norms is taken as an indication of the *cohesiveness* of the group.

group cohesiveness

informal norms

formal norms

Formally constituted groups, such as work teams, in which some of the norms, rules and goals for their members' behaviour have been established prior to their recruitment and interaction also evolve informal norms and forms of behaviour. Some of these may interfere with the formal norms and demands of the organization. Thus, incentive schemes, for instance, may be ignored by group members informally agreeing to restrict their output (as was demonstrated in the famous Hawthorne studies (Roethlisberger and Dickson, 1939)).

secondary group

The norms evolved in the primary group are usually the ones which govern the individual's behaviour whether or not such norms are in accordance with those of the larger secondary groups of which the smaller primary groups may be a part. (The term 'secondary group' has been used by social psychologists to describe larger and usually formally constituted entities such as factories, schools, political parties and clubs.)

There are several reasons why people may be more likely to adhere to the standards and expectations of their immediate primary groups. For one thing, these standards and expectations can be readily perceived within the primary group. For another, conformity to group norms brings psychological rewards through the acceptance by and support of other members – that is, if we assume that there is a need in human beings for attention or a response, whether such a need is innate or has evolved from early experiences of dependence and attachment to others (see Units 3 and 4). A further reason for adherence to the norms of members of one's immediate primary groups is based on the capacity of group members to exert pressure on deviants through withdrawal of affection, verbal admonitions or abuse and ridicule, physical assault, exclusion from the group (such as 'sending a member to Coventry') or 'blacking' someone's work. Such pressures may be directed towards a person's *behaviour* rather than her or his *attitudes*, since behaviour is visible whilst attitudes can be kept private. How far norms are upheld by members (in other words, how cohesive the group is) depends on the *meaning* which the group has for them, the opportunities they have of joining other groups and the reasons for joining a particular group in the first place. In exchange theory terms (see Unit 10/11, section 3) an individual will want to balance the *psychological cost* of changing behaviour or opinions to conform to the group with the *psychological reward* of being liked and accepted by others in the group.

ACTIVITY 1

List some of the *primary groups* of which you are a member.

Can you think of any instances in which you have modified your views or actions to fit in with the expectations of other members of these groups? Have you ever experienced a clash between membership of one group and that of another (such as between family and friends)? Do you exhibit (and experience) different facets of yourself in these different groups?

1.2 Membership and reference groups

In the last section we explored the formation of norms in the context of a series of laboratory experiments. In this section I want to review another study carried out in the 1930s in which Newcomb (1952) studied the changing attitudes of students towards public issues, not in the laboratory but in the 'real-life' situation of a residential college. This study, too, continues to interest social psychologists, firstly because it uses the concepts 'membership group' and 'reference group' which are still part of our current social psychological vocabulary, and secondly because further insights were gained when the students he studied were surveyed again twenty-five years later.

membership group
reference group

The term membership group simply refers to a group of which people are members by virtue of their presence in it. In contrast, the term reference group was first used by Hyman (1942) to refer to groups with which individuals compare themselves in evaluating their status. The concept, however, became part of social-psychological terminology through its use by Newcomb (Newcomb, 1952) in discussing his findings concerning attitude change among the students at Bennington College, outlined in Box 2.

Box 2 Membership and reference groups in a college for women students (Newcomb, 1952)

Bennington was (and is) an expensive East Coast American residential university college for women students. At the time at which the study was carried out (in the 1930s) most of its students came from wealthy conservative families. On arrival at the college these girls on the whole held conservative political views, that is, they had a pre-existing set of norms, but during their four-year stay at Bennington they were exposed to the more liberal (radical) attitudes of the teaching staff and senior students. There was a deliberate emphasis in the college on the discussion of a wide range of social problems, partly because this was a time of many stresses (the Depression) and attempts at social change (the New Deal), and partly because the teaching staff felt that, quite apart from any academic subject that students might study, they should become acquainted with the problems of their contemporary world.

As a result of these policies and attitudes of the staff, most of the girls underwent a marked shift in their attitudes, from relatively conservative to relatively liberal views, over the four years of their stay in the college. This is perhaps what one might expect in a fairly closely-knit, relatively small community (250 students) with an active liberal leadership. However, since not *all* the students changed their views in the expected direction, the effect cannot be attributed simply to the physical presence of a person in the group. In other words, the fact that Bennington College is a girl's *membership group* does not in itself explain the shift in opinion towards the 'prestige' attitude in the college. The crucial variable appears to be whether or not the student adopts the college community as a *positive reference group* for her own political attitudes. Interviews revealed that those girls who took the community as a *negative reference group* (that is, they felt hostile to it), and the home and family as a positive reference group for their political attitudes, remained unaffected by the liberal ethos of the college and continued to be conservative. They tended to have only a few friends at college. For some, the college was a positive reference group as a social focus but not a positive point of reference for political attitudes (and these girls did not change their outlook either but they did make many friends). Among those whose attitudes did change, the college was a positive reference group for political views; their parents may or may not have come to be viewed as a negative reference group: that is, some students took the college community as a reference point for their political attitudes without necessarily distancing themselves from their parents.

positive reference group
negative reference group

Why some of the students continued to take their home and family as a positive point of reference, whilst others took their new membership group as a positive point of reference, is a separate question and was not explored by Newcomb. The terms 'membership group' and 'reference group' are basically descriptive rather than explanatory concepts. Essentially, those who remained unaffected by the majority views in the college either had well thought-out conservative opinions (as opposed to merely 'complying' with parental views) or they were, in Newcomb's rather value-laden estimation, 'over-dependent' on home and parents. In a few cases they simply had other interests and made neither their home and family nor the college a point of reference for their attitudes.

The vast majority of the students did alter their political outlook and Newcomb thought that *in a different group they might have changed in a different way*. He concluded that attitudes are not acquired in a social vacuum and that attitudinal change is a function of how an individual relates her- or himself to the total membership group and to one or more reference groups. We might add, however, in view of the discussion in Block 5, that the probability of change also depends on the strength of the initial attitude and the discrepancy between one's own attitudinal position and that of people in one's new membership group. Furthermore, in 'yielding' to perceived group expectations, personality differences may play a part.

Newcomb, nevertheless, concluded – from the fact that most girls did adopt increasingly liberal views and on the basis of in-depth interviews – that *it is 'normal' to make one's current membership group one's (positive) reference group.*

Some twenty-five years later Newcomb (1967) carried out a follow-up study. He found that very few of the women he contacted had reverted to the conservative attitudes which they held before they attended Bennington College. Both the women (and their husbands) tended to have markedly more liberal views than a comparable sample of American women of the *same* socio-economic level. These findings can be accounted for in three ways:

(a) the values adopted during their stay at Bennington were 'internalized' (Kelman, 1958);

(b) the four years spent at Bennington proved such a satisfying experience that the College remained a vital reference group and focus in their lives; and/or

(c) the persistence of liberal views was a function of later liberal associations (such as husbands and friends) who were themselves chosen partly because of these shared beliefs.

Although the distinction between 'membership' and 'reference' group is descriptive rather than explanatory, thinking about group membership in these terms may lead to further insights. For instance, a man may be a plumber and hence described as working-class. He, however, may think of himself as a middle-class businessman and vote Conservative. *Why* he does this requires further elucidation, but recognizing that 'objective' indices of occupation and class membership do not necessarily indicate a person's reference groups (and the image she or he has of her- or himself) is a useful beginning.

Box 3 outlines another very interesting study which also focuses on the relationship of membership and reference groups.

Box 3   Reference groups, membership groups and attitude change (Siegel and Siegel, 1957)

Siegel and Siegel also studied the effects of membership and reference groups on attitudes of women students in a residential university by comparing the effects on attitudes according to whether the student had or had not obtained accommodation in a residence of her choice. Their sample consisted of women students who had all been living together in their first year at university. They all wished to join a prestigious and snobbish hall of residence (which can be taken to be their reference group) for their second year but there were vacancies for only some of them; the rest had to join less exclusive residences. The researchers were able to show that over a period of time 'the imposition of a membership group does have *some* effect on an individual's attitudes, even when the imposed group is *not* accepted by the individual as her reference group'. This conclusion derives from their finding that those who joined the less prestigious residences lowered their scores on the authoritarian personality scale (see Block 5) and some even made their membership group their reference group for their third year, that is, they opted to stay put for their third year even when offered a transfer to the hall of residence they had previously chosen.

It is useful to keep Siegel and Siegel's finding in mind since other studies, such as the one by Sherif which we have discussed, as well as some we are about to look at, also demonstrate that even *temporary* membership groups can have pronounced effects on the participating individuals. From a methodological point of view we may note that the study by the Siegels is an example of a field experiment, that is, an independent variable was manipulated (in this case, whether or not a student obtained her preferred choice of residence) and the outcomes observed. By contrast, the research at Bennington College was a field study, that is, observations were carried out in a real-life context but the researcher did not introduce manipulations of his own.

field experiment

field study

Are the studies we discussed in section 1.1 and in section 1.2 compatible? At first sight the *contrast* between Sherif's and Newcomb's studies seems most marked. Sherif's groups are artificial; the subjects do not have norms about the situation into which they are plunged; they form temporary groups; the groups are face-to-face. Newcomb's groups are real groups; the subjects have norms (political attitudes) which are relevant to their situation; the groups are relatively long-term; and two kinds of groups are considered, membership and reference groups (and the same group may be both a reference and a membership group but not invariably so). The conclusions of both authors, however, are *compatible* and *similar*: they both stress the *importance of group membership*, Sherif to the formation and maintenance of norms, Newcomb to the change of attitudes. Newcomb further stresses that one's membership group (which can be large or small) tends to become one's reference group.

ACTIVITY 2

Spend a few minutes listing any groups you take to be your *reference* groups.

Do you find you have different reference groups for different aspects of your life? For instance, your family for certain values and behaviours, your work mates for other aspects? Are you aware of any clash or conflict between your various reference groups?

1.3 Group pressure

The studies we have already reviewed testify to the power of group membership in forming or changing the norms or attitudes of people. In both Sherif's and Newcomb's studies interviews with subjects revealed that they experienced doubts or felt under pressure, but their subjective experience was not the main focus of the research. Another series of classic and influential studies carried out by S. E. Asch in the 1940s, however, did focus on the psychological pressures experienced by an individual or a small minority who disagree with the opinions or judgements expressed by the majority. Asch's immediate objective was to study the conditions which induce individuals either to resist group pressures or to yield to them, even when the views expressed by the majority are perceived by the subjects to be *contrary to fact*. See Box 4.

group pressure

Box 4   An experiment on group pressure (Asch, 1952)

Asch asked a group of male subjects to judge which of three lines presented on a card matched a standard comparison line on another card. In each group there were seven 'confederates' of the experimenter and one 'naive' subject, that is, a 'real' subject who did not know that the other people present had specific instructions as to how to act. The naive subject was always seated so as to be the second last person to call out his judgement. (If he had been last, the manipulation might have been too

---

obvious.) Initially, the seven 'stooges' named the same (correct) line and so, of course, did the naive member of the group. But then the experimenter's confederates began to make incorrect judgements about which line matched the standard line and thus the true subject was faced with a conflict between the judgements expressed by the other group members (who had established their credibility in his eyes through their earlier correct judgements) and the information coming to him from his own senses. In the baseline experiment it was quite obvious which of the lines was the matching line: see Figure 2.

Figure 2 An example of the two cards shown to subjects

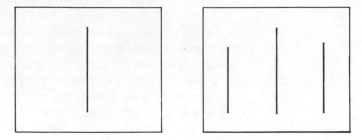

Source: Asch, 1955

majority influence

Subjects experienced bewilderment, tension and stress, but (and this is the question in which Asch was interested) did they yield to the majority's opinion or did they stick to their own judgements? In the basic condition described above subjects changed their responses in about one third of the judgements and answered in accordance with the group's false judgements. To put this another way, two-thirds of all the judgements were given without yielding to group pressure. However, there were great *individual differences:* one in four people never conformed, whilst others virtually always came to agree with the group. Post-experimental interviews revealed that the 'independent' subjects frequently experienced conflict or tension and doubt but they were resilient in shaking off oppressive group pressures. Others were able to isolate themselves mentally from the group and hence were also able to maintain their individuality. Post-experimental interviews also suggested that some of the 'yielding' subjects unconsciously distorted their *perceptions* – they actually 'saw' the lines in the way the stooges said they did. Most though, although they still saw the lines correctly, thought they must be misperceiving them and distorted their *judgements* to fit in with the group. A third category of yielders did not misperceive the lines, nor did they conclude that the majority was right; they yielded because of an overpowering need not to appear different from others.

Asch's experiments show that there are individual differences which lead some people to yield and others to remain independent (and you may well speculate on how you would have reacted!). The actual conditions of the experiment, however, also influence the outcome. Thus, in later experiments the difficulty of the task was increased by making the differences between the lines smaller. In this more ambiguous and confusing condition more subjects conformed to the group's judgements. When a subject was joined by another genuine subject, however, resistance to the views expressed by the other members of the group increased,

minority influence

even though the two were still only a *minority* in the group. (Much later, the study of how minorities achieve influence became a flourishing research topic: this will be discussed in section 1.6.) We may conclude from this series of experiments that whether individuals use the judgements made by members of their group for comparison purposes where they cannot independently verify their own impressions (for example, by measuring the lines) and whether they yield to them or resist them in making their own judgements depend on several things:

(a)   the characteristics of the stimulus, in this case how clear the differences are between the lines;

(b)   the group structure, in this case whether the subject is the only apparent deviant;

(c)   individual differences; and,

(d)   the cultural expectations of conformity that subjects bring to the experiment from their contemporary world.

Asch's experiments were widely replicated, usually with American college students as subjects. The results were fairly consistent and accord with the original findings though there were significant differences when people in a number of countries were tested. For instance, when Milgram (1961) compared Norwegian and French students carrying out this experiment, it was the Norwegian students who more readily agreed with the majority. More interesting, perhaps, is a more recent study by Larsen (1974) which demonstrated significantly lower rates of conformity in American students than Asch originally found. He attributes this to the changed climate of opinion which encouraged independence and criticism rather than conformity. Even more recently Perrin and Spencer (1981) found in a British study that in only one out of 396 trials did a subject join the erroneous majority though, like Asch's subjects, they experienced tension and stress. It must be pointed out, however, that their subjects were engineering, mathematics and chemistry students, well able to judge the length of lines and therefore in a strong position to resist psychological pressures to agree with inaccurate judgements on this particular task. I will come back to this point (that knowledge is a safeguard against pressures to conform) in section 1.5. Perrin and Spencer in the same paper also report rates of conformity approaching those of Asch when their subjects were young offenders on probation and the experimenter was an 'authority figure'. This does suggest that their and Larsen's student subjects (unlike the young offenders) were less in awe of their experimenters than were Asch's original ones (they called him 'sir' in interviews!) and that is, indeed, part of the cultural differences we are concerned with. People in the 1960s and early 1970s may have been more independent, questioning, critical or, perhaps, more knowledgeable about psychology (and hence more sceptical) than those in the 1950s and it is these characteristics which affect how they behave in the course of an experiment.

Larsen (1982) makes the point that a later study by himself and his colleagues (Larsen *et al.*, 1979) showed a return by the late 1970s to the levels of conformity found in the Asch situation in the 1950s. He explains this by stating that the *American* students of the late 1970s were again returning to the concerns of students in the 1950s and were more involved in preparation for jobs and careers than were their predecessors in the 1974 study who were motivated by social concerns and manifested lower rates of conformity. Larsen claims that the results suggest a relationship between broader social changes and laboratory conformity in that in the United States during the period of McCarthyism in the 1950s students exhibited high conformity, whilst the more questioning students of the Vietnam War era produced low conformity and students in the later 1970s again produced high conformity. Larsen further points out that during the last decade many students (by contrast with the 1960s 'activist' generation) joined mystical movements and religions which would also suggest less concern with independence and individuality. (We will return to this point again when discussing membership of sects in section 2.3.7.)

The results of such replications of Asch's experiment in different social climates illustrate the point I made earlier that social psychologists need to be aware of and take into account the 'societal level' of analysis even when studying intragroup phenomena. They may also illustrate that it is not only the subjects who have changed their attitudes in a changed climate of opinion but the experimenters, too, may have been affected and may no longer expect conformity to be demonstrated to the extent it was in Asch's original study. Hence, even when Asch's paradigm is apparently faithfully replicated, the experimenter may, unwittingly, convey to the subjects certain expectations as to the outcome of the **experimenter effects** experiment. Such unintended 'experimenter effects' are quite common and may present difficulties in interpreting the results of experiments (documented by Orne (1962) and Rosenthal (1966)).

These results also raise other, more worrying, questions about the validity of psychological research. If the same experiment can produce different results in different historical periods, are we to conclude that there are no universal 'truths' in social psychology? Is the validity of findings, whether derived from experiments or field research, always limited to the place and time where they were undertaken? The answer to both these questions is a qualified 'yes' in many areas of *social* psychology. However, the fact that social psychologists may not be dealing with universal truths does not make social psychological research either unimportant or uninteresting. It still helps us understand our own times and, where a topic has been studied over a period of time, the changes which have taken place in society and in the expectations and attitudes of people. Furthermore, where, for instance, we are trying to understand the nature of the *psychological processes* through which an individual is influenced, we may still arrive at valid insights even though the *extent* to which such processes operate may vary from one historical period or one society to another.

The search for 'universal truths' and the role of generalization in social psychology is discussed in the Metablock, Part III, paper 8.

1.4 Obedience to authority

Words such as conformity or compliance are concepts used in everyday life and they denote 'acceptance of influence'. Psychologists, as we have already seen, also use these terms and they have over a period of time endeavoured to define them more precisely, indeed to distinguish between them and to analyse the psychological processes which give rise to them. I will come back to these issues in section 1.5.

At this point we need first to review another series of psychological experiments in which a further term denoting 'acceptance of influence' was used. The studies were carried out by Milgram between 1960 and 1963 and brought together in a **obedience to authority** book (Milgram, 1974). Milgram used the phrase 'obedience to authority'. He distinguishes between obedience and conformity though he sees both as involving the abdication of personal responsibility. He views conformity as going along with one's peers in a group, whilst obedience is accorded to a person of authority in a hierarchical situation. Influence of one person over another, then, in this view arises from social power and status rather than from a psychological 'need' for acceptance by others. People usually deny that they conform (because of the value judgements attaching to this word) but they may be quite willing to make excuses for themselves by saying they *obeyed orders*.

Milgram considers obedience to be a basic element of social life and a determinant of behaviour of particular relevance to our time. His interest in obedience stems from the fact that millions of people were murdered in concentration camps during the Second World War, not necessarily by particularly evil men and women but through the operation of a bureaucratic process which depended on guards and others obeying orders. To explore how it was humanly possible for people to behave in this way, Milgram created situations in the laboratory in which the participants increasingly came into conflict with their consciences. These experiments are outlined in Box 5.

> ## Box 5 Experiments on obedience to authority (Milgram, 1974)
>
> Milgram set up a series of eighteen experiments in which he asked his subjects to act with increasing severity towards another person. The experiments were designed to explore the conditions in which they would or would not comply with the authority of the experimenter.
>
> The subjects, who were recruited by advertisements from a cross-section of the population to take part in a scientific study of learning and memory, were instructed to inflict increasing levels of electric shock on a 'learner' who made 'mistakes' in learning a series of paired words. Subjects met the 'learner', who was a confederate of the experimenter, at the outset. The 'learner' was then strapped into a chair in the next room and, as the experimenter proceeded, his cries of anguish and his pleas to stop the experiment could be heard. These were in fact pre-recorded and the electric shocks were not actually administered. The experiments were very realistically staged and each subject had been given a sample of the kind of electric shock he was about to administer.

Figure 3   Milgram's experiments on obedience

(a)

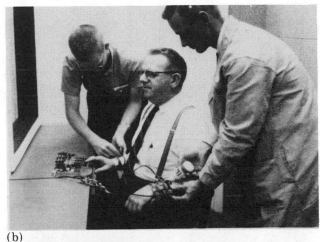
(b)

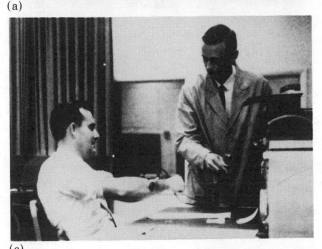
(c)

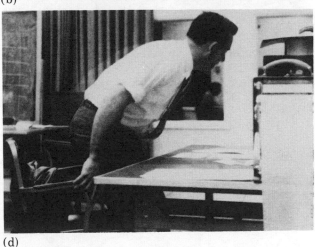
(d)

(a)   The shock generator used in the experiments. Fifteen of the thirty switches have already been depressed.

(b)   The learner is strapped into the chair and electrodes are attached to his wrist. Electrode paste is applied by the experimenter. The learner provides answers by depressing switches that light up numbers on an answer box.

(c)   A subject receives a sample shock from the generator.

(d)   A subject breaks off the experiment. On right, the event recorder wired into generator automatically records switches used by the subject.

Do you think you would have agreed to participate in such an experiment? Most people when asked this question reply that they would not agree to participate, nor do they believe that other people would be willing to do so. And yet many people did participate and twenty-six of forty male subjects in the original experiment administered the highest shock level on the generator, which was clearly marked 'dangerous'. The other fourteen refused to continue at an earlier stage.

The procedures in this and subsequent experiments required the subjects to offend against normal moral codes. Whilst the experiments created extreme levels of nervous tension, nevertheless, many subjects were prepared to carry on and accept (or at any rate act upon) the definition of the situation given by the experimenter, obeying him and ignoring the 'victim' although he too directly appealed to them. (In some of the experiments, the 'victm' was in the room rather than merely heard from the adjacent room and in these conditions fewer people were prepared to administer high levels of shock.)

In all, over one thousand participants came to be involved in these experiments. Most were male but forty women were also studied. Their level of obedience was virtually identical to that of the men. Milgram speculates whether this resulted from the supposed greater willingness of women to obey being cancelled out by their supposed greater empathy with people.

In the original design of these experiments group membership was not of prime concern. However, in some of them the subject became a member of a peer group. Thus, in one variation of the basic design, two confederates of the experimenter participated with the subject but were instructed to defy the experimenter's authority and refuse to punish the 'victim'. This experiment allows us to observe the extent to which support from fellow group members can release the subject from authoritarian control. The effect of the 'peer rebellion', as Milgram called it, was very impressive – thirty-six of forty subjects now defied the experimenter.

Milgram points out that a close analysis of the latter experiment reveals several factors that contribute to the effectiveness of the group in influencing the individual subject. He notes:

1   The peers instil in the subject the idea of defying the experimenter. It may not have occurred to some subjects as a possibility.

2   The lone subject in previous experiments had no way of knowing whether, if he defies the experimenter, he is performing in a bizarre manner or whether this action is a common occurrence in the laboratory. The two examples of disobedience he sees suggest that defiance is a natural reaction to the situation.

3   The reactions of the defiant confederates define the act of shocking the victim as improper. They provide social confirmation for the subject's suspicion that it is wrong to punish a man against his will [sic], even in the context of a psychological experiment.

4   The defiant confederates remain in the laboratory even after withdrawing from the experiment (they have agreed to answer post-experimental questions). Each additional shock administered by the naive subject then carries with it a measure of social disapproval from the two confederates.

5   As long as the two confederates participate in the experimental procedure, there is a dispersion of responsibility among the group members for shocking the victim. As the confederates withdraw, responsibility becomes focused on the naive subject.

6   The naive subject is a witness to two instances of disobedience and observes the consequences of defying the experimenter to be minimal.

7   The experimenter's power may be diminished by the very fact of failing to keep the two confederates in line, in accordance with the general rule that

every failure of authority to exact compliance to its commands weakens the perceived power of the authority (Homans, 1961).

(Milgram, 1974, pp. 120–1)

Thus, in a situation where subjects have support from others, they can resist external psychological pressures. We have already witnessed this in the Asch paradigm; in the condition where the subject was not the only 'naive' subject he was better able to resist group pressures and to stick to his own perceptions and judgements. In the Milgram experiments, when operating as a member of a peer group, the subject was able to oppose (or liberate himself from) the experimenter's expectations and authority.

One other experiment in this series of obedience studies is particularly relevant in the context of our discussion of the individual and the group. Milgram arranged this experiment in such a way that a confederate actually depressed the lever on the shock generator and the subject was merely engaged in subsidiary tasks. In this condition, thirty-seven of the forty subjects went on participating in the experiment to the end. As Milgram points out, they felt doubly absolved from responsibility – legitimate authority had given orders but they themselves had not committed any brutality.

What lessons can we learn from these disturbing studies?

In the Nuremberg trials after the Second World War, obedience by a soldier to a command resulting in an unlawful act was defined as a crime and this view has been generally accepted. In other words 'I was only following orders' is no longer considered an excuse for wrongdoing. For instance, those involved in the My Lai massacre in the later Vietnam war were not allowed to claim this defence. And yet Milgram's subjects carried out an odious task which could certainly be described as unlawful as well as immoral and they engaged in this task without being subjected to propaganda about the iniquities of the 'enemy' that is so characteristic of wartime situations. Ordinary decent people from all walks of life were quickly loosened from their moral moorings, did not act in accordance with their internalized values and engaged in barbarous acts because they perceived the experimenter as an 'authority' figure to whom obedience was due, even though they were appealed to by the 'victim' at the same time. (We shall return to the phenomenon of ignoring a person who needs help when we discuss 'bystander apathy' in section 3.7.) Whilst the subjects, that is, those who administered the shock, suffered from strain and anxiety and often asked to be allowed to stop, a high proportion nevertheless carried on. One way of explaining

denial   such behaviour is by reference to the Freudian concept of *denial* (a largely unconscious process which leads to the rejection of the evidence in front of one's eyes in order to arrive at an explanation which is less damaging to one's self-esteem: see also the Set Book (Stevens, 1983) p. 51). For instance, Milgram's subjects could deny to themselves responsibility for their actions since they could see themselves as merely following instructions; they might also blame the 'victim' for the situation (since he is making mistakes in his learning task and therefore has only himself to blame for the consequences).

The experiment I referred to earlier in which the confederate rather than the subject presses the lever on the shock-giving apparatus is perhaps the most disturbing. As Milgram points out, it parallels the kind of situation which had, initially, been the focus of his concern and which prevailed in Nazi Germany where a large bureaucracy cooperated in killing six million people in concentration camps though only relatively few engaged in the actual killing.

Set reading

You may now wish to read 'Problems of method' by Milgram in the Course Reader (Murphy, John and Brown, 1984). This chapter from his book (1974) discusses the methodological problems associated with taking a 'real-life' problem into the laboratory and whilst it is pertinent to this section it raises issues which have a wider relevance.

You can read this paper after you have worked through the Block if you prefer to continue with the present text.

1.5   Conformity and independence

conformity

What precisely do we mean by conformity? Does it imply unthinking or routine adherence to existing social values or forms of behaviour? Does conformity simply refer to the existence of a consensus about certain issues? We all, at times, conform in these senses, but conformity tends to become a 'problem' (and hence a focus of research) only when we think, possibly quite subjectively, that there is too much conformity or, and this is more important, when conformity leads to immoral or illegal actions and/or attitudes which are, apparently, contrary to an individual's 'normal' attitudes.

If you think back for a moment to the four major studies we have reviewed, you will remember that Sherif's study dramatically demonstrated the emergence of group norms and their retention by individuals even when no longer in the group. His work is important for that and, indeed, for establishing that it is possible to study the formation of social norms in the laboratory. Sherif did not use the word 'conformity' for what he observed though the behaviour of his subjects could be described as conformity to group norms (once they were established).

Newcomb's study is rather different from the others in that he observed a large group of people over four years and described the gradual change in attitudes which took place through debates and increased knowledge of social issues. Attitude change was described by him as a function of group membership for, you will recall, he considered it 'normal' to adopt the attitudes of one's group. Again the word 'conformity' was not used, the process being referred to as 'bending towards group expectations'. His work remains important for pointing out that group membership may have different effects according to whether an individual does or does not make a group her or his reference group.

captive audience

independence

With Asch we moved into a different league since he deliberately arranged laboratory situations to put group pressure on individuals to modify their own judgements. He did think of this both as conformity and as a deplorable attribute. He described his conforming subjects as *yielding* to group pressure. Had he thought of conformity as a positive trait, he might have referred to these subjects as *trusting* other people. Those who gave correct answers he referred to, approvingly, as *independent*. But, as has often been asked, do not the latter conform as well? They may continue to conform to the norms of their society in which after all two lines of the same length tend to be accepted as two lines of the same length. Hence, we can think of the naive subjects in the Asch situation as members of *temporary membership groups* in which some manage to maintain their links with their 'normal' membership and reference groups outside the immediate situation and others do not. These subjects are a 'captive audience' and, as we shall discuss in section 2.4.3, may in this respect be said to resemble prisoners of war who are subjected to propaganda and indoctrination. Do all of us then *always* conform but the apparent resisters conform to *other* groups or standards? This is indeed an unanswerable question but Moscovici and Faucheux (1972) hold that 'the only truly independent response in one of Asch's experiments was to leave the room' (p. 174).

When Allen (1975), however, carried out a study in which subjects had the option on each of twelve trials of *abstaining* from making a judgement, he found that subjects did *not* avoid the conflict by abstaining, that is, leaving the psychological field (if not the room), but rather exhibited the same degree of conformity as Asch's subjects. Allen concluded that a dual process is involved in group pressure – to answer rather than stay uncommitted because everyone else answers and, additionally, to agree with (that is, conform to) the group's position. Allen, too, found that, as in the Asch experiments, support for the minority was effective. In other words, when there was social support for abstaining because a confederate of the experimenter abstained, more subjects did, in fact, abstain. But we may both resist and conform at one and the same time in the same situation. Thus we saw in Milgram's studies on obedience to authority that subjects were better able to *resist* his authority when they had the opportunity to *conform* to the norms of resistance projected by his confederates.

Milgram, as we have seen, focused his attention on the effects of authority and distinguished pressure or support from fellow group members from the demands arising from a hierarchical context.

We will now turn to some other issues which follow on from the research already discussed and which will help us unravel the processes at work when social influence is accepted or rejected.

1.5.1 Public versus private acceptance

In discussing group influence a useful distinction may be made between *public compliance* (with the group norm, the majority opinion or the perceived expectations of the experimenter/leader) and *private agreement* or *private change* (from a prior attitude). Festinger (1953), Kelman (1958) and Jahoda (1959) have stressed the importance of making such a distinction. When an individual is exposed to group pressure, she or he may publicly conform or not conform to the group. Regardless of this public response, she or he can privately agree or disagree with the group. Hence the following are possible in response to group expectations:

(a) public conformity and private agreement;

(b) public conformity and private disagreement;

(c) public non-conformity and private disagreement.

(d) public non-conformity and private agreement.

(a) and (c) indicate a correspondence between public and private responses while (b) and (d) indicate a *lack* of such correspondence.

Two ostensibly identical responses of public conformity may thus reflect two quite different psychological states and, similarly, public non-conformity also may represent two different private states.

ACTIVITY 3

Can you think of examples which fit the above categorization?

Kelman (1958) has referred to public agreement without private change (that is, in the above terminology, with private disagreement) as *compliance* to group **compliance** norms for ulterior motives (to gain rewards or to avoid punishment). He further distinguishes *identification* with the group where agreement is public because the **identification** person values her or his membership of the group but the private acceptance is temporary and will not be maintained once the person leaves the group. A true private change is referred to by him as *internalization* and implies that an **internalization** attitude has become part of the person's own value system (because the new information or opinion fits in with her or his other attitudes). Once internalized, the attitude will be maintained even when the individual is no longer a member of the group. Festinger (1953) made a similar point. He argues that public conformity will be accompanied by private acceptance only if the person wants to remain a member of the group which is attempting to influence her or him. However, whether a person does or does not conform depends on many factors – is it a 'real' group or simply an experimental group with a short life? How attractive is the group to her or him? What other group memberships are open to her or him? Can she or he effectively leave the group? Is 'leaving the scene' a person's habitual way of reducing cognitive dissonance (a term you met in Block 5)? But is Festinger necessarily correct? We can all think of instances where we privately disagreed even though we wished to remain as members of the group. Thus I might disagree with the course team over an issue, maintain my private opinion (even after counter-arguments advanced by fellow members) and yet remain, and wish to remain, a member of the team. Of course, there is perhaps no genuine choice of leaving the course team since my own work is tied to this group for several years. One would have to have very fundamental differences to leave a group in such circumstances.

Is it possible to determine empirically whether a group produces only public compliance or both public compliance and private acceptance? One way might be to ask a subject to give a public verbal response and at the same time give a private written response hidden from the group. But, given that such a response would be seen later by the experimenter, from the subject's point of view it might not be a genuinely private response. Another method would be to compare the public response given under group pressure and the response when the group is not present. However, if both responses agree with the group one might still not be able to conclude that private acceptance occurred at the time when the public response was made. As we shall shortly discuss, private change may have occurred later through different psychological processes operating initially at a latent level (see section 1.6). There is, of course, also the possibility of interviewing subjects after experimental sessions, but here, too, memory may be incomplete or censored by the individual's conscious or unconscious attempts at maintaining her or his self-image. If you think back to Sherif's experiments on the autokinetic effect (in Box 1) you may conclude that he obtained lasting rather than merely temporary change in that his subjects carried the norms and ranges they developed initially into later experimental situations. Of course, as you also remember, the situation was totally ambiguous and subjects initially had no previous norms on which to rely or to which to return, once they were away from the group, and this is rather different from most other situations in which people find themselves.

Festinger (1957) in his cognitive dissonance theory suggests that attitude change may follow voluntary counter-attitudinal public behaviour since an action, once engaged in, cannot be undone. Hence, one way of reducing dissonance is to change one's view or attitudes and, therefore, the very act of public commitment may also produce private acceptance.

However, you will remember, in the Asch experiment (Box 4) the overt agreement with the group led to private acceptance in only a few subjects. His interviews showed that it was unusual for subjects to change their *perception* of the stimulus (which we might equate with private acceptance): they merely agreed with the group even though they thought the group was wrong. (And, of course, even those who reported a perceptual change may have 'rationalized' their agreement with the group which is another way of reducing cognitive dissonance.) There is confirmation of the temporary nature of the effect of Asch's procedure from Luchins and Luchins (1955) who found that when, after the group session, the entire set of lines was re-administered to the subject in the absence of the confederates, no mistakes occurred. This is, perhaps, not very surprising since it is difficult to imagine a private commitment to an issue such as which lines are equal to a standard line when the facts (in the absence of group pressure) are unequivocal.

Nevertheless, this point may not be entirely straightforward. Again it is Festinger who makes an interesting comment. According to his theory of cognitive dissonance, the attractiveness of the chosen alternative (in this case, to agree with the group) increases after the decision and the attractiveness of the unchosen possibility (in this case, to disagree with the group) decreases. This implies that a subject who has adopted a certain position may maintain this response during the experiment *and* in later experimental sessions. Though perhaps, if such a response pattern occurs, it need not be explained in terms of commitment – another emotive word; rather we may think of it as the formation of a response *norm* in the way that Sherif demonstrated. Such a response norm can also be viewed as face-saving and as reducing post-decision dissonance.

However, commitment to or involvement with an issue *prior* to any attempt at influencing the person, whether through group pressure or persuasive communications, may affect the outcome. Thus, Jahoda (1959) points out that 'one and the same position taken by different individuals can have completely different meanings, that is, different antecedents, different contexts, and different consequences'. She adds: 'position-taking on an issue in which the individual has intellectual and emotional investment is psychologically so different a process from position-taking on an issue which is not so invested, that they must be assumed to manifest different regularities.' In her analysis of the empirical work on conformity Jahoda alerts us to the danger of taking too simplistic a view of the process and its outcomes. Figure 4 shows the eight acts which can result from the influence process when a person's initial position is taken into account.

Figure 4   Types of conformity and independence (adapted from Jahoda, 1959)

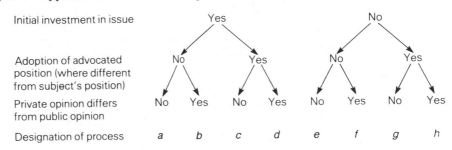

Explanatory comments:

a, b, c and *d* refer to persons with an initial intellectual or emotional involvement with an issue.

a   denotes a person who does not change her or his mind and is at ease with her- or himself about the final position she or he takes.

b   implies a person who adheres to her or his original position but feels less comfortable with it than she or he used to.

c   describes a person who changed her or his mind as a result of a campaign or group pressure and who is at ease with her- or himself.

d   describes a person who complies under some pressure but maintains her or his private opinion.

e, f, g, h refer to persons who had *no* intellectual or emotional involvement with an issue.

e   denotes a person not affected by a campaign or group pressure.

f   denotes a person who has changed her or his opinion privately only – on the face of it an unlikely position.

g   denotes a common response where there is no initial involvement in an issue.

h   denotes a person who maintains her or his private opinion even though there is no initial investment in the issue, a less common response.

ACTIVITY 4

Can you think of people and situations which fit some or all of these categories?

1.5.2 Public versus private response

So far I have discussed the relationship between public response and private acceptance without focusing specifically on whether a person's behaviour was observed in a public or a private condition though, where subjects had the opportunity to respond in public *and* in private, the private response was taken by psychologists as being indicative of the person's private acceptance. However, the question has been raised as to whether the *mode of response* itself will affect the issue. A *public response* would be a response given aloud in a face-to-face group, as in the original Asch experiment. The term *private response* generally refers to a response given anonymously and in private. You have had a well-known example of the disparity between a publicly and a privately given response in Block 5 when LaPiere's (1934) study was discussed. You may remember that in that study hotel-owners stated in response to a questionnaire that they would not accommodate Chinese people, but when they came face-to-face with a Chinese couple very few refused to do so. You were given several explanations for these differences. An individual may have a range of attitudes on a given issue and different situations may elicit the display of only some of them. On the other hand, the *mode of response* (filling in an anonymous questionnaire as compared to having to make a decision on what to do in a face-to-face situation) may also affect the response. Some studies have been undertaken by social psychologists where the mode of response has been made the independent variable. Thus, for instance, Levy (1960) studied conformity in a face-to-face situation and in one where the alleged responses of other group members were shown on a screen but the subject was on his own and gave his response in private. Levy found more conformity in face-to-face groups than in the simulated groups and so did other researchers. However, it is not obvious what one is to make of such results. Two possible interpretations can be put forward: either that people conform more on public occasions to avoid disagreements irrespective of their private views, or that a face-to-face group may simply be more convincing than simulated responses. Hence the fact that the response is given in relative privacy may be irrelevant and may not produce the observed variations in conformity in the two conditions.

1.5.3 Personal predisposition versus situational determinants

The original Asch studies, whilst emphasizing the situational factors which affect conformity, have also shown that individuals vary in the extent to which they conform to the group. Similarly, research on responses to persuasive communications (discussed in Block 5) has also demonstrated some individual differences in susceptibility to influence.

However, a good deal of research on demographic and personality factors, designed to pinpoint the psychological characteristics of individuals who may be predisposed to yield to or to resist influence from group members or from persuasive communications, has not led to any clear-cut results. For instance, it has been asked whether age and sex have something to do with a person's persuasibility. Age, except in the first few years of life when children tend to accept influence more readily than later, does not appear to be a very significant variable. As regards sex, in so far as any differences are found, some studies showed that women were somewhat more easily influenced than men (Hovland and Janis, 1959). However, such findings may be of historical interest only and no longer true, given that the self-esteem and self-reliance of women is greater than it was twenty years ago. Sistrunk and McDavid (1971) have also shown that the results in earlier studies were an artifact of the items chosen: when the subject matter was familiar to women, they did not conform to the incorrect majority views and, indeed, the same is true of men. Appropriate knowledge, as we have also seen in discussing Perrin and Spencer's (1981) replication of the Asch studies, reduces the susceptibility of both sexes to false majority opinion. Investigations of the role of intelligence have given contradictory results, not perhaps surprisingly, since an intelligent person may be more capable of paying attention to and comprehending persuasive information but may also have the knowledge or alertness to resist yielding to it. Characteristics such as a person's degree of self-esteem or anxiety (often temporarily manipulated and changed by the experimenter) also produce a confusing picture when related to her or his susceptibility to influence. Again, the internal mediating processes may work against each other: anxiety may make a person more prone to yield to persuasion (see Block 5) or group pressure but less susceptible because she or he fails to pay attention or because anxiety may hinder comprehension.

The focus on personality factors has been virtually abandoned because of a growing awareness that yielding or remaining independent do not represent unitary character traits which an individual either possesses or lacks. More fruitful insights have been gained by focusing on the situational aspects which may determine the *extent* of the group's influence. Thus, psychologists have studied the size and unanimity of the group; the cohesiveness and attractiveness of the group; the individual's status (do leaders conform more or less to group norms? – see section 2.2.6); the extremity of the norms presented (the more extreme the norms, the greater the conflict in the deviant subject); the nature of the task (visual stimuli as in Asch or opinion or information items); and, as has already been mentioned, the subject's competence (the more competent at a task the subject is, the less conformity occurs). Similarly, in Block 5 your attention has been drawn to a number of factors (beyond predisposition) which affect the extent to which conformity to persuasive communications is achieved. Thus the structure of a communication, the credibility of the communicator, the type of issue, and the channel through which the communiction is presented were all shown to affect the outcome. I want to remind you also that the evidence and discussion in Block 5 have demonstrated the importance of taking into account both an individual's primary groups and the wider social system when looking at the way in which individuals react to influence attempts. For instance, Hovland *et al.* (1953) stressed the *salience* of group norms to the issue presented. (Group norms are salient to an individual if they are the norms of her or his *reference groups*, to use the terminology employed in the present Block.)

non-conformity

Much of the research following on from Asch has focused on conformity, its nature and the conditions in which it is most likely to occur. But, quite early on, in fact in Asch's first series of experiments, non-conformity was explored. Thus, as we discussed in section 1.3, when one other member of the group gave the correct response, the naive subject's ability to resist the erroneous majority was considerably increased (Asch, 1951).

Can we define non-conformity? In an ideal world I would be able to give you agreed definitions of such terms as independence, non-conformity, anticonformity or dissent. However, these terms, like the concept of conformity, have been as variously employed by psychologists as by people in general. Disagreement with the group may indicate a spirit of independence, or conformity to a partner in the group, or conformity to reference groups beyond one's immediate membership group.

Allen (1975), amongst others, has carried out a series of experiments on the factors affecting independence from group judgements. His particular focus was the effect of social support for the subject's *private* beliefs and perceptions. The stimuli he used ranged from visual items to opinion and knowledge statements. He concluded that the response a subject gives is largely determined by the *meaning* he ascribes to the situation. In his view, conformity is reduced because the social support a subject receives from a partner instigates a process of cognitive restructuring that results in a different interpretation of the stimulus. Thus one important function of the social supporter (or partner as Allen calls her or him) may be to provide an independent confirmation of physical and social reality when the subject is confronted with anomalous behaviour from the group. In this way, the subject's dependence on the majority for information and rewards is reduced, as is his conformity to the majority. The subject's relationship with her or his partner also influences the outcome. Both Asch (1955) and Allen and Wilder (reported in Allen (1975)) set up experiments in which the partner 'deserted' the subject and began to agree with the group halfway through the experimental session. In both sets of experiments this led to increased conformity to the group by the subject after the 'desertion'. Allen explains these results by arguing that, initially, the credibility of the partner had increased as a consequence of her or his agreement with the subject. When however, the partner begins to agree with the group, the group is re-evaluated and *its* credibility is increased.

Both a person's disposition and situational variables would appear to determine the *degree* of an individual's dissent from or agreement with a group. Thus, it is virtually impossible to classify behaviour as conformist or independent *unless* one understands the meaning the situation has for the individual (as Jahoda (1959) had already pointed out) and the implications it has for her or his self-image. Allen concludes that the person's ultimate response is the outcome of the balancing of situational factors (the support she or he has, the ambiguity and nature of the stimulus and so on) and her or his initial perception or opinion. One might add that the meaning an experimental or real-life situation has for people also depends on their goals: are they trying to achieve the completion of a task, the solving of a problem and/or do they wish to be popular or successful?

1.6   Majority and minority influence

In the preceding sections we have seen that a minority of two (as compared to a lone individual) is better placed to *resist* the influence of the majority in a group and remain independent. However, in 1969 the preoccupation with conformity gave way to a new question: how can an individual or a minority not just resist the majority but *influence* it? This question has generated considerable research and theorizing in the last fifteen years and research is still continuing (including at the Open University).

minority influence

It is interesting to speculate why there was such a change in focus among social psychologists. Whilst one can point to a group of prominent European social psychologists – Moscovici and his colleagues – who initially posed this question and used an experimental situation which could be readily replicated, this alone would not explain the widespread interest which this question raised, particularly in Europe. Perhaps the changing social climate which we already identified as affecting the responses of subjects in the Asch paradigm also affected the interests of social psychologists.

In their first experiment Moscovici, Lage and Naffrechoux (1969 (see Box 6) were able to demonstrate that a consistent minority is able to exert a remarkable degree of influence even when it lacks such characteristics as power, status, competence or idiosyncrasy credit (Hollander, 1964; see section 2.2.6).

Numerous studies since have supported the main finding of these experiments that consistent minorities will exert influence whilst inconsistent behaviour will not bring about a change in the majority's perceptions or points of view.

passive minority
active minority

How can we account for the effects produced by a consistent minority? Moscovici and Faucheux (1972) first of all distinguish between passive and active minorities. The former occur in the dependency relationships in the laboratory, where the individual or the minority is isolated and overwhelmed by uncertainty: such situations do, of course, also occur in life – prisoners in solitary confinement and victims of hijacks are effectively cut off from their wider society and usual frames of reference. However, there are also active minorities who are sure of their opinions and determined to press for their acceptance: such groups may emerge after periods of oppression. The black power movements or the declaration that 'black is beautiful' are recent examples of a minority actively involving itself in social change. Original thought, innovation, reforms or revolutions would not be possible without deviants or minorities who propose alternative goals or means. Such minorities can become the instigators of social change, as we shall see when we discuss the genesis and effects of *social movements* in Unit 22. Here I want to make one point which directly relates to minorities *within* groups.

Schachter (1957) has shown that a deviant who asserts her or his position attracts most of the communications from others in the group, their aim being the re-establishing of social cohesion and unanimity. But the deviant individual or the minority can use these efforts by other group members to argue back and make them choose between the 'deviant' and the 'group' response. Moscovici and Faucheaux (1972) point out that the consistency with which a position is maintained and, more generally, the 'behavioural style' of a minority are factors which may weaken the majority, in part because the minority thus demonstrates that alternative viewpoints are possible. Moscovici and Nemeth (1974) suggest that the consistency, commitment and autonomy of the minority lead the majority members to revise their opinion of the minority and to question their own position. This may lead to the minority having a (perhaps disproportionate) influence on the majority. Nevertheless, behavioural style, however defined, is only one ingredient. It is likely to mesh with other factors such as the knowledge group members have about an issue. A contemporary British example of a consistent, committed and autonomous minority is the Militant Tendency within local Labour Party groups. This example also lends support to the point made earlier that dependency on the majority is, in part at any rate, a function of the confusion and normlessness of the individual in the typical conformity experiment. The Militant Tendency, by contrast, do not lack strong convictions or consistency or, for that matter, reference groups outside the immediate membership group.

conversion
compliance

Moscovici (1980) elaborates on his findings concerning the influence of minorities and further suggests that the influence of the minority may be at a latent rather than at a manifest level. He describes the former as conversion, the latter as compliance (without inner conviction). He emphasizes that both minorities and majorities exert influence, that the views of the former are not automatically rejected because they are contrary to the majority's norms, nor are the views of the latter accepted without resistance because they agree with the norm. If no change can be observed in response to a minority position on a direct, outward level, some alteration may nevertheless have taken place on an indirect, latent level and may become manifest later. In other words, the minority's views or actions may raise doubts and dissonance which continue to work in the mind of the individual. In that way, he hypothesizes, the latent 'conversion' processes initiated by the minority may have a greater effect on a 'deeper' level than the overt, and possibly temporary, 'compliance' effects resulting from the influence of the majority.[1] A shift in emphasis has hence occurred from *interpersonal* influence processes to *intrapersonal* cognitive processes operating over a period of time. This shift also implies a greater awareness of the complexity of the processes involved and a change of focus from control and conformity to change and innovation. Thus, the research on minority influence in groups has proved to be a corrective to the earlier concern with conformity.

As we have already seen, majorities and minorities seem to have different effects *and* seem to work through different processes. The information coming from a minority source is likely to be processed more *actively* (because it causes cognitive and social conflict and generates more counter-arguments); the information coming from the majority is processed more passively (since the fact of there being a majority is hypothesized as making the minority dependent on the majority and they will 'unthinkingly' accept its influence). This has been referred **dual process model** to as the 'dual process model', that is, it rests on the assumption that minorities and majorities produce qualitatively different effects through different underlying processes. There is support for this view from experimental studies (for a review, see Moscovici (1980)).

But why should the minority and the majority produce such different effects? It is likely that being faced with a majority with whom one disagrees is more stressful than being faced with a minority, because in the first case (for instance, in the Asch situation) an individual faces both a challenge to her or his own position *and* the likelihood of disapproval from the majority. By contrast, the minority does not have this kind of immediate impact and is less threatening, and thus the majority may be more willing and able to consider the minority's point of view. Nemeth and Wachtler (1983) suggest that *majority* influence will lead to the minority either following the majority exactly or remaining independent. They hypothesize that where the influencing agent is a member of a *minority*, subjects will reassess their positions, will be under less stress and may be likely to *adopt a novel position*, that is, one which is different both from their own original position and the one advocated. In their experiment subjects were asked to resolve an embedded figures task (that is, find figures which are hidden in the overall design). In both the conformity and the minority paradigm the confederates always found the same two embedded figures. The subjects in the former complied with the majority, in the latter condition the subjects were less likely to name these two embedded figures but found a great number of additional figures which had not been proposed by the confederates. In other words, the challenge posed by the minority led others in the group to think for themselves and the authors suggest that this experiment shows that the influence of the minority can lead to creativity and innovation.

However, the 'dual process model' has not remained unchallenged. Latané with various co-workers (Latané and Nida, 1980; Latané and Wolf, 1981) has proposed **social impact theory** a theory of social impact which may account for the reciprocal influence of majorities and minorities in laboratory settings. Previous work, as we have seen, has suggested that the influence of the minority and the majority require different explanations. Thus the impact of the majority can be viewed as resulting from its greater ability to establish social reality and from the dependency of the minority on the majority. The influence of the minority has been attributed to its consistent behavioural style (perhaps its only weapon), denoting confidence and commitment and thus becoming the focus of attention.

Social impact theory, by contrast, hypothesizes that one common influence process is responsible for both conformity and minority influence. Rather than taking the group as a whole, it views the majority and the minority as separate sources of influence in the same social field. Each of these sub-groups (or a single individual) is seen as a potential source of influence for the other. Whatever position an individual assumes with respect to a given issue, she or he will be an active participant in the influence process and the influence of majorities and minorities is seen as simultaneous and reciprocal. Thus, where majorities and minorities are of comparable size one would expect that any emerging consensus would be less one-sided than it would be if there were no minority position advocated. Unlike Moscovici's model, however, social impact theory does not suggest that the minority's influence will be more than proportional to its strength, nor does this theory address itself to the question of whether and how an individual or a minority can maintain their original position. Going beyond the laboratory, Latané and Wolf (1981) note that the influence of the minority is based on the fact that in changing times and conditions the views of the minority may be more realistic than those of the outmoded majority. They thus may serve as the trigger to the 'conversion' effects identified by Moscovici (1980). As they put it: 'Like the child who first remarked on the Emperor's lack of clothes, non-elite minorities may be effective mainly when majorities have blinded themselves to naked reality. If the Emperor were in fact dressed the child would, of course, be ignored' (Latané and Wolf, 1981, p. 452).

Whatever theoretical formulation has been used to explain minority influence (such as the dual process model or social impact theory), consistency has emerged as the main thrust of the minority. However, consistency has not always been clearly defined in the many experiments where it featured. Furthermore, its effects depend on the perceptions of the target group who tend to *attribute* confidence, competence, certainty and distinctiveness to the consistent minority.

Their attributions may also hinge on other factors. A good deal of research has demonstrated that consistency is a necessary but not a sufficient condition for minority influence to occur. For instance, a very rigid rather than a flexible style of argument or a large discrepancy between the position advocated by the minority and the target majority may cut across the effects of consistency and affect the outcome.

If you think back over this section you may conclude that minorities are potentially very effective change agents, producing private change rather than overt compliance and that such change is brought about by intense cognitive activity. This would be a fair conclusion and yet we can see all around us the continuing effects of pressures towards conformity. Two points can be made.

First, these experiments were designed to explore minority influences, the circumstances in which they became apparent and the cognitive and other processes through which they created their effects. However, such explorations do not nullify the experiments which showed how conformity comes about; they merely demonstrate that minority influences can *also* be brought into play.

Secondly, some authors have pointed out (for instance, Mugny, 1982) that by agreeing with the minority a person runs the risk of being identified with it and thereby assuming a minority status. If the problem put to a group is a realistic one, this is an important consideration and may make people hesitate to adopt a minority opinion. The kind of realistic issues which Mugny, a Swiss psychologist, used were attitudes to 'guest-workers' and to compulsory military service. We might, therefore, again expect some differences according to whether in the experiment the *mode of response* was public or private; also, even though people hesitate to join a minority publicly, they may still be affected by the *conversion* processes hypothesized by Moscovici. In the world at large, of course, there is another factor: arguments on important issues, such as (in Switzerland) the position of 'guest-workers' or compulsory military service, do not occur just in a one-off laboratory experiment. The issues are widely debated in the media, in pubs, in the family and among friends. The ultimate outcome, therefore, cannot be pinpointed in a laboratory experiment. However, to demonstrate that minorities, in the laboratory or in life, can stimulate a rethinking is both interesting and worthwhile.

Finally, we need to note that all the laboratory research referred to here has dealt with experimental groups in which the minority has been instructed on how to behave so the effect on the 'naive' subjects could be studied. Research on experimental juries (such as Sealy, 1975) in which the split between the majority and the minority is not predetermined and controlled have pointed to the complex interactions which take place in the jury room. In the research described by Sealy, groups of twelve people listen to a tape-recording based on a real trial. Each member of the jury privately notes whether she or he thinks the defendant is guilty or not guilty and then the jury members proceed to discuss the evidence with a view to arriving jointly at an agreed and publicly stated verdict. Sealy found that it was not possible to predict the group's verdict from the size of the initial majority in favour of a guilty or not-guilty verdict.

ACTIVITY 5

Are you a member of any kind of group which discusses issues on which members are encouraged or required to take a stand or make a decision? Such groups could be policy-making groups, staff meetings, committees or a group of parents organizing a play group. If so, think back to recent meetings (or observe at a forth-coming meeting) and analyse the interplay between a deviant opinion-holder or minority and the majority. Which way does influence flow? Or is it multi-directional? Does the size of the minority matter? Do the status or behavioural style of either the minority or majority seem to matter? Is there pressure towards consensus? Do you think any changes you observe in opinions are due to 'confor-mity' or 'conversion'?

Your observations may not be conclusive but they may illuminate the discussion in this section.

1.7 Conclusions to section 1

group We have seen that the word 'group' refers to many entities: to large or small, formal or informal groups; to groups in which a person is present or groups taken as a reference point whether or not an individual is physically present in them; to ephemeral experimental groups or groups which have a long history; and to groups which a person joins voluntarily or is thrust into by birth or nationality. Whilst the word 'group' is used in all these contexts it might be more correct to refer at all times to 'people in groups' or 'people relating to each other in groups' or some such form of words. The word 'group' reifies (literally: makes a thing of) something which does not exist except in terms of the effects those participating (by their physical or mental presence) have on each other, the meanings they attribute to such interactions and the intrapsychic cognitive restructuring which may result. But, as Jahoda (1982) points out, though 'we are all unique individuals . . . no experience, thought, feeling or achievement is conceivable as the creation of a single mind'. Thus, even though we may have ceased to look on groups as *things* – out there to be observed or participated in – they are still a meaningful focus in social psychology, and, having made the point concerning the danger of reification, I shall continue to use the word as a shorthand reference to the relationships of people in groups.

The word 'member', too, can have different meanings for the individual concer-ned. How fully people consider themselves to be members of a group (and hence likely to be influenced by others in the group) may depend on the group's structure, the context in which it exists or evolves, the extent to which mem-bership in other groups is available to them, their dispositions and knowledge.

The effects that group membership is likely to have (on perceptions, attitudes, values, judgements or behaviour and so on) depend on the characteristics of the group as they mesh with the needs or characteristics of its members. The intra-group effects may also be affected by the wider social context in which they occur. The precise outcomes of such interactions are, therefore, difficult to predict. The observed outcomes, as we have seen, are also, in part, an artefact of

36

the particular questions one asks – such as whether one is concerned with the conditions in which conformity occurs or with the exploration of independence or deviance. Furthermore, the precise manipulation of the independent variable and what is accepted as the dependent variable (for instance, a response in private or public) also affect the outcome.

Because of the complexity arising from the interplay of all these factors it is not possible to decide which of the influence processes we have discussed is most fundamental. Thus, social comparison processes, conformity pressures, the stimulus emanating from strong minority opinions or the view that 'social impact' owes something to all participants, all describe processes for which there is experimental evidence and which may go on *simultaneously*. The focus on any one of them results from the (necessarily) partial view a researcher or theorist takes. The first and last of these processes are, of course, more inclusive and probably can be applied to the understanding of most ingroup behaviour and experience. The others arise more specifically from the issues to which their proponents have addressed themselves.

We have seen that the questions social psychologists have asked about the effects of group membership have changed over a period of time. Questions concerning the formation and maintenance of individual and group norms (Sherif, 1936) were followed by the exploration of the effects of membership as compared to reference groups (Newcomb, 1952). The psychological experience of group pressure (Asch, 1952) proved a focus for much subsequent research both on conformity to and (relative) independence from group norms and a shift in emphasis from interpersonal influence processes to intrapersonal cognitive restructuring.

Underlying all these questions and the different influence processes which have been identified, there are basically two aspects of groups which underpin the explanations given for the effects which group members have on each other (and they are not mutually exclusive).

The first kind of explanation derives from the observable fact, discussed in Block 1, that we are born with predispositions and attributes which mark us out as social being and that our early dependence on other people for survival strengthens and develops such dispositions. In this sense it is 'natural' that we seek out others, congregate with others (even when, as I pointed out in the introduction to this Block, there is no practical necessity to do so) and, the corollary to such assumptions, adjust to other people as well as expect other people to adjust to our views, preferences or behaviours. Social life would not be possible unless this were so and this is what is encapsulated in the study of 'groups'. As I have pointed out in section 1.1, the importance of the concept of group rests on the fact that primary groups arise spontaneously (and can very easily be established even in artificial laboratory situations). Where they exceed more than about twelve members, they tend to split into new groups as they become too large for all members to have face-to-face contact. It is no accident that groups in which cohesion is important rarely exceed a dozen members – Christ's disciples (and here one member became a deviant), the cricket eleven or a football team all testify to this fact. At the Open University we have found that where course teams have more than a dozen or so members, a core team tends to emerge to reduce tensions and facilitate cooperation.

power   The second kind of explanation focuses on the power relationships within groups. Thus, the majority in a group may be perceived as powerful 'norm senders', since **sanctions**   they have sanctions at their disposal (disapproval or rejection). These sanctions are effective in producing the outcomes desired by the majority precisely because deviant or potentially deviant group members are assumed to be psychologically dependent on the majority for information and/or approval. In this sense, an explanation in terms of power is entirely compatible with stating that 'we bend towards group expectations' (Newcomb, 1952) because it is human nature to be social and to adopt the attitudes of the group or groups of which one is a member. But, as we have seen, when one focuses on the influence of the minority, then one cannot speak of power but one needs to have recourse to describing its effect in terms of a chain of cognitive restructuring processes. The concept of power tends to refer to position, status, privileged access to information or the weight of numbers, that is, the resources which make sanctions possible. In that sense, minorities do not have power and, insofar as they are effective, achieve influence through stimulating rethinking in the majority.

Power is primarily a sociological concept, referring to aspects inherent in the social structure (such as class divisions or the system of apartheid). In section 2 I will return to this point when we discuss leadership, a word which denotes success in the psychological procesess of deliberately influencing others; this process is frequently associated with and, indeed, at times is dependent on, the power arising from a formal position in a social hierarchy. Experimenters, of course, are also often in a position where they are seen as leaders: they set the scene by devising the experiment; they represent 'science' and they are 'in the know', unlike their *subjects* – a very revealing word in this context; and they may have a formal position in the hierarchy of status and power as lecturers or heads of department and have 'real' sanctions at their disposal, such as a requirement for students to put in a certain number of hours as experimental subjects to gain a 'credit' for their course.

social control
social influence

When we refer to power in the sense of having a privileged position in the social structure, it might be better to refer to the exercise of power as social *control* rather than as social *influence*. The latter arises in the interaction between people and is a much more inclusive term and independent of whether or not there are asymmetric power positions in the group. It is the word used throughout this first part of the Block (and in the literature on which it is based). However, these two terms are not so far apart as one might imagine. Social control is not only based on power but on using 'normal' social influence processes to attempt to change the attitudes or behaviours of people in a predetermined direction. This will be the topic of section 2 of this Block. Before turning to section 2, however, we need to take stock of the progress we have made.

First of all, can we now define the concept of group?

I do not think that we can give *one* definition. We have seen that there are many different kinds of groups and that research has largely focused on the influence processes at work, whether these are intra-individual or inter-individual. These in turn are affected by the wider context in which the group occurs (the societal level) and structural aspects of the group itself, whether these derive from the societal level or are imposed by the experimenter, who might, for instance, arrange an experiment so that minorities and majorities with asymmetrical power relationships are created in the laboratory situation. If you care to look back to the definition of a group by Shaw (1971) in the Block introduction then you can see that, at the most, it may be applicable to the 'social impact model' discussed in section 1.6 but not to anything else. It has the merit, however, of properly *defining groups in terms of ongoing influence processes, rather than as a thing with given properties*, even though we need to refine the all-embracing statement Shaw makes.

Many recent textbooks do not give a definition of groups but are prepared to define aspects of groups or group membership such as group norms, group structure or group cohesiveness. Where a definition is advanced it is often immediately challengeable. For instance, Barton *et al.* (1974) define a group as: 'Two or more individuals who are interdependent on one or more dimensions and who perceive the existence of the group and their membership in it.' Whilst we would need to define 'interdependent' to make sense of the first part of this statement we know that the second part is wrong: influence processes *can* be at work without the individual being aware of this – a matter demonstrated as early as the 1930s by Sherif's studies on the formation of norms. It is, of course, true that people mostly are conscious of being members of groups – of reference groups, such as 'the British' or '*Guardian* readers', or of membership groups (which, possibly also serve as reference groups) such as a team, or a family or a self-help study group.

The evidence for their membership derives from their sharing, or coming to share, *common norms* about issues of importance to them whether or not they are aware of this process. This is why I opened our study of groups with Sherif's study of the development of norms. If no such consensus arises over a period of time, the group will not maintain itself as a *meaningful psychological focus* in its members' life. A group may in such circumstances maintain a formal existence (such as an empty but non-dissolved marriage) or it may disintegrate (though mainly in the short-term, as we have seen, people may conform overtly to group norms (compliance) and maintain their private views). We have also seen that where there is a felt need for change a group may evolve new norms in their interactions (Nemeth and Wachtler, 1983).

Given the difficulty of defining groups other than in terms of the influence processes at work or in terms of important characteristics such as shared norms, I would prefer to think of groups as an *area of study* whose boundaries are blurred and where not all findings can be immediately or obviously reconciled with each other. Thus we saw that cognitive dissonance theory may lead one to expect that public conformity will lead to private change (Festinger, 1953). Conversely, Moscovici (1980) in exploring minority influences came to the conclusion that private change (conversion) can take place *without* any change at the public level.

Even if we cannot adopt one definition for the concept 'group', we still need to ask whether in studying groups we have uncovered issues or processes or entities which differ from those discussed in earlier parts of the course. For instance, you may wonder whether *groups* are different from *dyads* or *triads*. We can speak of two- or three-person groups, hence the difference does not lie in the size of these entities. The difference lies in the questions which researchers have posed and the assumptions they have started from. If you think back to Unit 2 on family processes, you can readily see that the researchers and theorists who figured there, addressed themselves to issues which were different from those we explored here. Similarly, I have in all these pages never used the word 'imitation' though you may feel, thinking back to Unit 4 and the discussion there of social learning theory, that compliance or conformity may imply imitation and may depend on reinforcement (another word not used by group theorists).

Theories develop, in part, in response to societal problems or issues and their exponents borrow from everyday language certain words which they then define in technical ways. Perhaps all one needs to say is that 'imitation' and 'conformity' 'belong' to different schools of psychology. Imitation is mainly part of the vocabulary of the behaviourist social learning theorist (though it has been used by other psychologists and sociologists, as we shall see in section 4) and tends to be used to describe *individual behaviour*, whilst conformity has been the concern of those social psychologists (many of whom were refugees from European dictatorships in the 1930s which demanded more conformity to their political views than they were prepared to give) who became interested in *group processes* – though, of course, it is still the *individual* who conforms to or resists the standards and expectations of others in the group.

Finally, just to keep your adrenalin flowing, I would like to leave you with a paradox. We have seen that small face-to-face groups form spontaneously and hence may be considered an essential part of normal living. Helping an individual to form relationships with others should, therefore, have beneficial consequences: neurotic patients, for instance, may be helped to face their problems and take their first steps back towards normal relationships by the support and sympathy they receive during group psychotherapeutic sessions from others, similarly burdened. Well known, too, are the methods of groups such as Alcoholics Anomymous: alcoholics, wishing to shake off their dependence on drink, can meet others who have faced the same problems and they can unburden themselves in talking to them; furthermore, they will be supported in their endeavour to stop drinking by a small group of helpers who are available to them on request at any time of day or night. Membership of a group of 'weight-watchers' similarly gives an individual the moral strength to abstain from excessive eating.

Studies from industry show that labour turnover is often particularly high in the first weeks of employment. This may be due to a variety of factors, but firms which have made special efforts to integrate newcomers into their organization and into their work-groups find that they can considerably reduce the numbers of those who leave (and hence not only make savings on the cost of recruitment and training but increase the satisfaction of individual staff members who succeed in their jobs rather than leave).

But, and here is the paradox, the group may also be viewed as the *cause* of stress or mental illness. A particular school of psychiatry (including Laing, 1970) thinks of mental illness not as something which is 'located' in the individual, rather the origins of mental illness are seen as the result of faulty interactions in the patient's primary groups, particularly, as you have already witnessed in Unit 2, in the family. This may be precisely because it is so difficult for some individuals to seek a way out by leaving the family and its tangled web: we may be eternally attracted by those who destroy us.

2 GROUP MEMBERSHIP AND SOCIAL CONTROL: FROM GROUP DECISION-MAKING TO MASS SUICIDE

The fact that we are affected by those with whom we interact has inevitably led to the *use of group situations as potent forms of social control and social change*. Such attempts to deliberately change the attitudes or the behaviour of group members will be the focus of this second section of the Block, in contrast to the first section where we were concerned to establish through what processes and in what circumstances members of a group, or of subgroups such as minorities and majorities, influence each other.

It must be obvious that attempts to change people raise serious questions. First of all, there are scientific questions concerned with establishing which measures, if any, are effective in changing people in given contexts. Secondly, the very research process through which the above questions might be answered may be fraught with ethical problems; for instance, people may be put under great stress in order to observe whether they have a breaking point. And thirdly, assuming that we have confidence in the validity of the scientific findings, there are ethical issues in implementing them. In particular, even if attempts at changing people stem from benevolent intentions, great care needs to be taken as even good intentions do not necessarily result in beneficial outcomes. Change-agents, that is, people such as politicians, teachers, family planning advisors, health educators, agricultural extension officers and social workers, should therefore repeatedly question their motives as well as their methods, even though, as we shall see, change-agents often tend to be less effective than they hope to be in achieving their goals. We shall be concerned with these three sets of questions in this section.

2.1 Decision-making in groups

In a moment we are going to discuss several studies carried out by Kurt Lewin, a German-born psychologist who emigrated to the United States in the 1930s. He was one of the psychologists whom I had in mind when I wrote at the beginning of section 1 that early social psychologists had a strong interest in applying their findings to social reform and social policy, for Lewin is often quoted as saying, 'There is nothing more practical than a good theory'. He was the first to engage in **action research** 'action research', that is, research where the researcher intervenes in a situation and then monitors the effects the intervention produced. (This should be con- **participant observation** trasted with participant field observation where a researcher takes part in the events she or he observes but without, it is hoped, affecting them by her or his presence.) Lewin founded the Research Center for Group Dynamics in 1944 at the Massachusetts Institute of Technology and the Commission for Community Interrelations of the American Jewish Congress in 1945. He initiated much research into prejudice, discrimination and intergroup relations, including industrial conflict. Even though he died in 1947, when only in his fifties, he has had a tremendous and continuing influence on social psychology. This can be attributed not only to his ability to test theoretical ideas experimentally and to promote action research but through his students and associates, many of whom became leaders in American social psychology. Some have been mentioned already in this course, among them Heider, Festinger, Schachter, H. H. Kelley, Deutsch and Cartwright. (You might like to trace these influences in the Metablock, Part III, paper 1.)

One of Lewin's major interests was the study of group dynamics. We will first look at his research on group decision-making. As we shall see, he came to think that it is easier to induce social change by involving groups, rather than by persuading individuals directly, and to do so by encouraging group members to discover relevant facts for themselves through discussion with others in the group. He thought of reason as a social value and equated reasoning and democracy because 'it grants to the reasoning partners a status of equality' (Lewin, 1948, p. 83). How did he come to evolve such views?

During the Second World War Lewin carried out a series of studies to explore how housewives could be induced to change their food habits so as to drink more milk and to give their babies orange juice and codliver oil. In these studies he tested the efficacy of presenting information to group members either through a lecture or through eliciting such information through group discussion, the latter method arising from his profound faith in the virtues of democracy. This study is outlined in Box 7.

Box 7   Group decision and social change (Lewin, 1947)

One such study (Lewin, 1947) was carried out in 1943 when the US government was anxious to get housewives to serve cheaper cuts of meat to their families. Two methods were used. Three groups of between thirteen and seventeen Red Cross volunteer housewives attended interesting lectures which linked the problem of nutrition with the war effort, emphasized the vitamin and mineral content of offal and stressed health and economic aspects. The preparation of dishes was described and recipes distributed.

In three other groups, composed of the same kind of people, a nutrition expert introduced the same topic and then let the group members discuss the issues. In such a discussion, the expert helps the group with factual information but refrains from telling people what they should do or think or how to overcome their dislike of offal. At the end of the discussion period, members were asked if they would serve kidneys, hearts and so on during the following week and the same recipes were distributed.

A follow-up showed that only three per cent of the women who heard the lectures served one of the meats never served before, whereas after group discussion and decision thirty-two per cent served at least one such meal.

How can one explain these effects? One possible explanation is that people tend to resist authoritarian pressures but are willing to accept new ideas from their peers. Perhaps the to and fro of discussion allows people to test the appropriateness of various ideas and gives them the feeling that they have convinced themselves and made their own decisions. This process can generate considerable involvement as contrasted with more passive listening to a lecture.

A second reason for the more ready acceptance of new ideas in the discussion groups in these experiments may be the fact that in these groups each member was asked to make a *decision* about her own intentions. (Such individual decisions may be contrasted with those made by juries or committees who make decisions as group members rather than as individuals. In such situations, discussions may need to be continued till a *consensus* is reached.)

The issue of the importance of actually making a decision was taken up by Pelz (1958) who demonstrated that two factors were instrumental in bringing about the changed perceptions and intentions of the members of discussion groups. One, a new *shared group norm* evolved during the discussions and became *apparent* to the participants; and two, the act of *making a decision* of one's own choice, whether privately or publicly, led to the commitment to carry it out.

What are some of the wider implications of these studies?

Making a decision may convert something external – the proposal of the discussion leader – into something internal, a conscious choice. With no decision, the suggestion is likely to remain external. Unlike a mere group discussion, a group decision should lead to setting up definite goals for action. These goals may be set up for the group as a whole or by each individual in the group for her- or himself. But the group discussion and the communication between members is likely to lead to their involvement with the issue and with the subsequent decision. The group decision, in contrast to the influence of a lecture, thus implies a conscious stand on the part of an individual.

ACTIVITY 6

Think back to the discussion in Unit 17/18 on the effects of the mass media compared with interpersonal influences and relate them to Lewin's experiments. Can we compare the lecture to mass media influences and the discussion group to the interaction of the opinion leader with her or his group? Think back to an occasion when you bought a new product. How did you come to take this decision? Were you influenced by the mass media? Friends? Discussion with other people? Or how?

We may or may not agree that it is a good thing that housewives can be led to convince themselves that they contribute to their country's war effort by changing the dietary habits of their families. When we return to the effects of group discussion in a later section, we will see that this same process can be used to achieve results that are morally questionable. Even in Lewin's study, we need to remember that the scene is set by the group leader and that the 'ideal' outcome is predefined by her or him. The aims are to effect a change in the direction desired by the leader and to make the change acceptable to the participants. Group discussions and group decision-making are (in cases such as this) an attempt at social control (or 'social engineering' as Lewin called it approvingly), albeit possibly a more acceptable means of control than issuing and enforcing orders. An alternative to persuading people to change their eating habits would presumably involve rationing and laws against blackmarketeering with punishments meted out to those who break the law. Following on from Lewin, group discussions have been used in factories and have been shown to be effective in getting groups of workers to overcome their resistance to changes in work practices desired by management (for example, Coch and French, 1948). However, we need to note that such 'participation' by workers is likely to be effective (from the point of view of the management) only if there are no fundamental economic or ideological differences between the workers and the management. Where both management and workers desire the *same* ends, for instance increased productivity, then group discussions and decisions will utilize the workers' knowledge and may enhance their pride and commitment.

You may have your own views as to whether such efforts at making the exercise of authority less autocratic by fostering conditions through information and discussion in which the individual and the work-group may identify with the objectives of an organization and participate in the decision-making process are an attempt at democratizing decision-making at the work-place. Some critics hold that this approach is 'manipulative' since, far from lessening managerial control, it may make its exercise more effective: organizational objectives will have been understood and more readily accepted and, hence, control by the managerial hierarchy will also be supported by peer-group pressures.

The emphasis upon groups and the desirability of involving individuals in change has, since Lewin's death, led to such developments as T (for training) groups, later called sensitivity groups. These groups are led by a relatively non-directive but sensitively observing 'trainer' with the intention of giving participants insight into their own motivation and behaviour. Indeed it was Lewin who founded the National Training Laboratories at Bethel, Maine, where these groups originated, but he died before the work got into its stride.

Related to these later developments and Lewin's original work there has been in recent years a growth of various self-help movements such as Alcoholics Anonymous and smoking clinics which are intended to help individuals to help themselves. Such self-help groups tend to have predetermined aims (for instance the members of a group of weight-watchers want to shed surplus weight) but membership is voluntary and the individuals joining such groups have themselves taken the initiative in seeking to effect a change in their behaviour or attitudes (though you may feel in the case of groups of weight-watchers that they have been 'manipulated' by the media to think that being slim is important). Such groups, too, tend to be chaired by an expert who gives advice on diet. Members *decide* publicly on their own targets of weight reduction and it is the approval and support of members which help each individual to reach her or his goal. Whether such group-based methods of self-persuasion can be thought of as aiding personal growth and self-control is a matter of opinion. Some people move from one such group experience to the next, or from one type of encounter group to another, without apparently finding either salvation or even a modicum of happiness, integrity as a person, or an increase in competence in dealing with everyday life. Others have been able to stop smoking or overeating or have found satisfaction in developing new insights and guidelines for their lives.

Recommended reading
You might like to read now or at some later stage the excerpt in the Course Reader from Ehrenreich and English (1979) entitled 'For her own good: 150 years of expert advice to women'. This excerpt is reproduced in Chapter 5 which discusses, amongst other things, the conditions in which popular psychology flourishes and why there has been an upsurge of interest in 'personal growth'. The authors are critical of the human potential movement and, whether or not you agree with them, you may find this extract refreshing and thought-provoking.

Group discussions need not merely be a method of engineering consensus (though this is our focus in this section). They also provide the possibility of pooling knowledge and skills in finding solutions to problems (be they design problems in industry or a case conference of social workers). They need not be chaired by someone with a predetermined aim. They can be fairly unstructured as in 'brainstorming' sessions though there is controversy over whether such methods do, in fact, foster creativity. Whilst here I have focused on the effects on members of *making* a decision individually or as a group, there is also considerable research (and controversy) on how groups *arrive* at their decisions. Is group decision-making a matter of information being shared, as discussed in section 1.6, or are social comparison influences more crucial? Do groups make more extreme decisions (group polarization) than individuals on their own, or does the pressure to reach consensus lead decision-making groups to overlook important evidence with the result that they produce erroneous or low quality solutions – a phenomenon

group think named 'group think' by Janis (1968)? Consensus is comfortable and people may shut their minds to evidence of changes in the environment which require investigation and decisions. Thus it has been shown that neither the attack on the American Fleet at Pearl Harbour (Wohlstetter, 1962) nor the Argentine invasion of the Falklands should have been unexpected (Franks, 1983). These two examples from the political sphere have been well documented but if you work in any kind of organization you may be able to think back to decisions taken there which placed too much emphasis on consensus and neglected opposing views or information with the result that these decisions were impracticable or untenable in the long if not the short run.

So far we have looked at some aspects of group decision-making and, more or less in passing, have made reference to group discussion leaders (or experts or trainers) who help the group to arrive at its decisions. Such leaders are only one of the species, one we shall in the next section learn to refer to as 'democratic' leaders but, as we shall see, there are also other types of leaders.

2.2   Leadership

The study of leadership has a long history as a research theme reflecting changing interests in social psychology as well as changing perceptions of a leader's role in society. Having got as far as you have in this course, you will appreciate that social scientists tend to define the problems they investigate in terms of the theoretical framework and the empirical traditions in which they work and, as a consequence, may ignore aspects which are of concern either to the layperson or to social scientists adhering to different schools of thought. However, there is another potential source of bias. Social scientists tend to research problems very much in the way in which they have been presented to them by those who pay for the research. For instance, the study of human relations in industry has been largely financed by management or institutions supported by the government rather than by trade unions. One may well speculate as to the questions trade unions would have posed had they thought of financing research. Whilst the point I am making about the funding of research is quite general and pervasive (as has also been pointed out in Block 5), it is of special relevance to research on *leadership* which has often been commissioned and financed by the military and by management. Research is not necessarily invalidated because it is sponsored, but one ought to be aware that the research may have been coloured by its original purpose.

2.2.1   Early studies of leadership

Early work on leadership attempted to identify the personality characteristics which successful leaders have in common but such research invariably showed that successful leaders could have widely different traits and attributes. Just think of, say, a military commander and an abbess in charge of a convent; or the leader of an expedition bent on conquering an unclimbed mountain peak and a leader of a discussion group. All these are leaders but they may need quite different personalities, aptitudes or skills. The point to note is not that personal qualities and relevant knowledge are unimportant but that it has proved impossible to make a list of attributes or traits which fits a wide range of leaders without considering their qualities *in relation to the situations and problems they face and the membership of the group in question.* Nevertheless, as we shall see, 'personality' in various guises has come to the fore from time to time in leadership research.

2.2.2 Leadership style

leadership style

Leaving these early researchers aside we can turn to a pioneering study of leadership which was carried out by Lewin and his colleagues (Lewin *et al.*, 1939) who focused not so much on a leader's personality as on her or his leadership style. For Lewin, the crucial determinant of group atmosphere lies in leadership and the style adopted by the leader: see Box 8.

Box 8   Research on leadership style (Lewin *et al.*, 1939)

Lewin, as a refugee from totalitarianism, was concerned to establish the superiority of the 'democratic' method of leadership. To this end he arranged for three groups of boys and girls to join a club to make masks after school hours. One group was led by an 'autocratic' leader who issued orders; the second one was led by a 'democratic' leader who got the children to discuss what they wanted to do and how to achieve their objectives; the final group worked with a *'laissez-faire'* leader who was present but did not initiate any action. The leaders for these groups were not chosen by dint of their 'democratic' or 'autocratic' or *'laissez-faire'* personalities. They acted the way they did because Lewin told them to present a particular *leadership style* to their groups.

The democratic group always met two days before the autocratic group. The democratic group chose its activities freely and whatever they had *chosen* to do, the autocratic and *laissez-faire* groups were then *told* to do. In this way there would be a basis for comparing the 'output' of the children as well as their experience and behaviour.

Lewin found that the 'productivity' of the first two groups was quite comparable but the children in the autocratic group were dissatisfied and some of them became aggressive (to each other rather than the leader) and resentful, whilst others retreated into apathy. In the democratic group there was a good deal of cooperation among the children and they enjoyed the group. The *laissez-faire* group was neither very productive nor particularly satisfied. Lewin subsequently told the leaders to change their original style and it was again the style which affected the outcome in the various groups. The fact that a leader can be instructed to adopt a particular style implies that managers or officers or other leaders can be helped, through training, to adopt a style which corresponds to the expectations of their group members. Lewin also changed two of the most aggressive children from the autocratic to the democratic group where they quickly became cooperative members who enjoyed the after school clubs. The lesson here is, as the British Army has so graphically expressed it long before these studies took place: there are no bad soldiers, only bad officers.

These results, of course, need to be understood in the context of the social climate in which they took place, a context which favoured democracy above autocracy. If these experiments could have been carried out in Nazi Germany the result might well have shown that the children were more at ease in the 'autocratic' group. This reservation on the general validity of these studies makes a very important point – that individuals, their groups and leaders can only be understood in the context of the wider society of which they form a part. School clubs, the army, industrial or any other kind of organizations cannot, ultimately, be studied as if they were closed systems. The style of leadership which is acceptable (and hence, other things being equal, effective) is intimately bound up with the norms prevalent in the wider society. The participants in organizations occupy roles outside the organizations which serve as a basis for their level of expectations within the organization and for the social comparison processes which determine their perception of the equity or inequity of any transaction within the organization.

2.2.3   Selection of army officers

Lewin's research had no direct influence on the changes which took place in the British Army's methods of selecting its officers during the Second World War but the changes described below developed out of similar concerns.

In the British Army, officers used to have to buy their commissions, but even when this practice was stopped they tended still to be recruited from the public schools. A radical change took place during World War II when the supply of potential officers from such a narrow stratum of society proved insufficient in both quantity and quality. With the help of psychiatrists and psychologists new methods of selection were developed. In addition to being interviewed by psychiatrists and taking batteries of psychological tests (to ensure that these potential officers were 'normal'), candidates were put into groups which faced the kind of problems junior officers might have to deal with. These situations required cooperation but there were no obvious solutions; indeed some had no solution, which increased the stressfulness of the situation. What mattered to the selectors was not so much the quality of the ideas individuals put forward but how they related to other people in the group, whether a person's suggestions were adopted by the other group members and carried out or whether an individual opted out or perhaps became inflexible when frustrated.

These selection procedures were so successful that they are essentially still in operation and are, in a modified version, also used for the selection of civil service administrative trainees (the 'country house method') and for management trainees.

The army candidates so selected did well in their officer training courses and subsequently in the field. The method was also more acceptable to potential candidates and appeared to be more 'democratic' than selection by interview. One of those who participated in developing these group-based selection methods was W. R. Bion who later became a pioneer of group psychotherapy (Bion, 1961).

situational determinants of leadership

Stemming in part from these group-based methods of selection, research on leadership switched in the 1950s from the identification of personality characteristics to *situational determinants* of leadership effectiveness. The main thrust of this approach was to highlight the dependence of the leader upon her or his group. This is virtually the opposite of the approach which locates the leader's power within her or his personality. The situational approach equates the leader's status with her or his ability to command liking from the group and deal with its immediate problems. In time, researchers became aware of the limitations of this view, and adopted, as we shall see, a perspective on leadership which looked on it as a complex social process, a transaction or exchange among members of a group. This new perspective or model posited that the nature of the task, the structure of the group and the expectations and perceptions of the followers all influence the process of leadership.

2.2.4   Leadership in industry

During the 1950s and early 1960s there was still considerable interest in the notion of leadership style, particularly in the effects which a supervisor's or manager's leadership style had on those they organized. Sayles (1966) reviewed both experimental and survey studies on styles of leadership. He found the emerging picture inconsistent; no superiority of one style over another was demonstrated in the *experimental studies* of supervisors though *survey studies* revealed the greater acceptability and productivity of 'democratic' over 'autocratic' leadership. Sayles contends that the tasks in the experimental studies were of such a boring and limited nature (and in that, of course, they resembled many industrial tasks) that people did not become involved and variations in leadership style had relatively little impact. Sayles makes the point that supervisors who use a 'democratic' leadership style probably also differ in other ways from their more 'autocratic' colleagues. He thinks the former might be more intelligent (since some of the research on the authoritarian personality (Adorno *et al.*, 1950) has shown a correlation between low intelligence and high scores on scales which indicate authoritarian attitudes). If 'democratic' supervisors are more intelligent then, clearly, they can deal better with both production difficulties (which may affect wages) and with 'human relations' problems. It seems very obvious that a supervisor needs to address both these issues and, yet, industrial social psychology in the 1950s and 1960s seemed to be almost wholly preoccupied with the notion that managers need to be 'people-centred' rather than 'task-centred' (this stance, of course, was a reaction to the previous overemphasis on technical aspects of the supervisor's job).

people-centred versus task-centered leadership

In the 1960s, in parallel with the above emphases, there was again a resurgence of interest in the personality characteristics of the leader though in novel terms. Fiedler (1967, 1968, 1971) was initially interested in the inclination of the leader to distinguish between his most and least preferred co-worker (LPC). His researches showed that leaders who see their LPC in a relatively favourable light tend to be more accepting, permissive, considerate and *person-oriented* in their relations with group members. The person who sees her or his most and least preferred co-worker as quite different and the latter in an unfavourable light tends to be directive, controlling, *task-oriented* and dominant in her or his interactions. Fiedler then developed (and tested in several countries and in different organizational contexts) his *contingency model* for the analysis of leadership effectiveness. He sees the effectiveness of the leader as *contingent* on the fit between her or his personal qualities and her or his leadership style (whether 'relationship-oriented' or 'task-oriented') on the one hand and the needs of the situation on the other. Thus, his model predicts varying levels of effectiveness for different combinations of leader and situational characteristics. Fiedler distinguishes three situational variables which influence the leader role:

contingency model of leadership

(a)   the quality of leader–member relations, that is, the extent to which the leader has the confidence of her or his group and, more generally, the psychological climate of the group;

(b)   the task structure, that is, the complexity and clarity of the task and the number of solutions which are possible: the more unstructured the task, the more the leader must inspire and motivate people rather than rely on backing by *her* or *his* superiors;

(c)   the position power of the leader, that is, the power inherent in her or his position, the rewards and punishments at her or his disposal and the organizational support on which she or he can depend.

Fiedler predicted that the managing, controlling leaders perform most effectively either in very favourable or in very unfavourable situations. Considerate, permissive leaders obtain optimal group performance under situations intermediate in favourableness such as where the leader is liked but has an ambiguous, unstructured task and must therefore draw on the knowledge and cooperation of group members. Fiedler re-analysed data from his earlier research and also carried out a major experiment to test his model. Both yielded considerable support for this theory. Fiedler's data thus support the idea that leadership effectiveness depends not only on the characteristics of the leadership style and the personal attributes of the leader (such as the ability to make discriminating judgements of group members) but on their *relevance* to the needs of the particular situation. Situational factors, such as the task structure, the degree of power the leader has, and the leader-member relations, affect what form of leadership ('permissive' or 'autocratic', 'people-' or 'task-centred') is likely to be effective. Fiedler's findings (that organizational structure or technology – the task structure – define the appropriate personal style) parallel the conclusions to be drawn from the work of Woodward (1965).

Joan Woodward showed, by comparing eighty firms variously engaged in unit or small batch, large batch or mass- and flow production that the technology of manufacture influences the organizational structure of the firm and that the structure, in turn, profoundly affects the relationships between managers, supervisors and workers. She found in her study that the technology of production influences such aspects of management as the degree of centralization of decision-making, the degree to which standard procedures can be established, the extent to which specialist services are developed and the ratio of managers to workers and the style of management.

Trist and his fellow workers (Trist et al., 1963) at the Tavistock Institute of Human Relations took a somewhat different line. They showed that one need not take a technological system of production as 'given' in a situation, from which then follow certain organizational consequences and effects on relationships at work. When a new technological system of coal-mining (the so called long-wall method) was introduced they were able to design work practices which did not disrupt the strong group cohesion (which is a feature of mining work) and which continued to meet the social and psychological needs of the miners and yet achieved superior economic results. Thus both Woodward, and Trist and his colleagues (and others, too) found, like Fiedler, that it is not very useful to study leadership (or management) except in relation to other aspects of a situation.

Fiedler's 'theory of leadership effectiveness' provides a complex and elegant model embodying both *situational* variables, such as task structure and power position, and *psychological* variables, such as the leader's ability to make discriminating assessments of fellow-workers as well as her or his preferred leadership style. Fiedler, incidentally, thinks of a person's leadership style as a relatively stable personality attribute, whereas earlier work by Lewin and his colleagues (Lewin et al., 1939) discussed in section 2.2.2 suggested that a leader can be taught to adopt a new style though this need not necessarily imply a change in outlook and deeply held attitudes. Some people may well use a leadership style which is not a true expression of their basic attitudes but is a 'copy' of the models of leadership style they themselves have been exposed to or which corresponds to the style of colleagues or the firm's policies. Whether or not changing one's style is easy or possible depends, therefore, on a variety of antecedent as well as current factors.

Fiedler, as we have seen, is interested in exploring whether different leadership styles are appropriate for different situations. In other words, he is interested in the 'fit' between the psychological and situational variables. Far from suggesting, however, that leaders should be encouraged to change their style of management to fit the situation, Fiedler (1965) suggests that we must learn how to 'engineer' the job to fit the leadership style and the needs of managers who happen to be available. His grounds for stating this are that intelligent and technically competent people are in short supply, that training is costly and time-consuming whilst a little thought would allow one to place people into situations compatible with their 'natural' leadership style. Selectively used, this approach might well be fruitful in some situations. It should be possible, at times at any rate, to change both task structures (as Trist et al. did) and the power position of the leader. The third situational variable, that of the quality of the group–leader relationships, cannot be easily manipulated, or indeed, precisely operationalized and assessed. It might itself, of course, be influenced, if not in the short run then in the long run, by the leader's style. The perception of the leader's legitimacy will be influenced by the extent to which she or he meets the normative expectations of her or his co-workers, including their expectations concerning the leader's competence to meet their task or socio-emotional needs. The expectations of the group members as to their preferred style of leadership mesh, probably, with the task structure and their own motivation. An individual will 'judge' a leader's actions and motives in accordance with her or his own needs for job satisfaction and/or other rewards, such as bonus payments which may depend on the organizational ability of the leader/manager.

Interestingly and rather surprisingly in view of the fact that he earlier thought of a leader's style as a relatively stable attribute, Fiedler in a later paper (1972) suggests that leaders themselves have varying needs and goals and they might, therefore, vary their behaviour and adapt to the situation in which they find themselves. 'Controlling' leaders might become 'relationship oriented' and leaders who employ a 'permissive' style might use a 'controlling' style when they operate in situations which make a different approach more effective or which allow the satisfaction of needs which are of only secondary importance in other situations.

Fiedler, therefore, seems to be suggesting a new element of indeterminancy in his model. Although he specifies what he considers to be the relevant inputs in the leadership situation, he appears to be qualifying the nature of these 'givens'. None remains absolute and he describes a truly interactive process in which both leaders and led may adapt, and task and power structures can also be changed. This, of course, means that it is impossible to predict the directions in which the system might move – at least, in terms of this particular analytic framework. If Fiedler's suggestion that the situation can be 'engineered' to fit the leader and her or his style of leadership is feasible then, equally, it should be possible to 'engineer' situations to fit the needs and capacities of other participants in the interests of personal satisfaction as well as efficiency or productivity. Fiedler, however, is concerned with leader effectiveness (in getting the job done). Unlike Lewin, he does not address himself to the question of whether a particular style of leadership also aids the satisfaction of co-workers' needs nor does he concern himself explicitly with the perception of the leader by the followers. I think this imbalance in the model, or, rather, the neglect of the variable of reciprocal perceptions, is probably due to the assumptions made in the model that a leader tends to have a formal position which provides her or him with legitimacy and varying degrees of power (and hence the perceptions of the followers do not matter as much as the leader's skill in assessing co-workers). This is often the case and a relevant starting point to take in writing about leadership effectiveness, but leaders can be challenged, deposed or ignored (in organizations as well as everywhere else) and new leaders may emerge to deal with new situations or to fill needs not met by the former leaders. It is, of course, also true that when a leader has come to the fore, say in an unofficial strike, she or he will try, if the problem is not quickly solved, to create an aura of legitimacy for her- or himself by getting explicit support from followers for carrying on the struggle. Such 'unofficial' leaders gain support when they meet the needs of their followers better than 'official' leaders, be they managers or trade union leaders. Incidentally, in laboratory experiments it has been found that elected, as opposed to appointed, leaders feel freer to disagree with their group members (Hollander and Julian, 1970). This might suggest that the elected members were more secure in their status (at least for the time being).

The style of leadership that leaders adopt may vary with their perceptions of the psychological situation in which they find themselves and it is, therefore, not necessarily a stable personality characteristic. Thus an 'autocratic' field commander of a guerilla force may eventually become a 'democratic' and constitutional head of his country. Whether or not leadership style is a personality characteristic, control (or leadership) in organizations is based both on power (inherent in a particular position) and on legitimating approval from subordinates, peers and superiors and hence tends to conform broadly to commonly held norms and expectations on how such authority is to be exercised. The leader is part of this context, not outside it.

2.2.5 Communication networks and leadership

From a quite different line of research we have some evidence which supports the idea that leadership is not an inborn personality characteristic. These studies show that when people are put into positions where the group needs to depend on their efforts they tend to rise to the challenge and behave as leaders and are also recognized by others as such. These findings derive from studies in which a communication network is imposed on experimental groups. Left to their own devices, groups naturally evolve their own communication structures. (This is illustrated by Figure 11 in Unit 6, a sociometric diagram which charts the interactions of members of a gang.) Research on imposed structures (such as **communication networks** Leavitt, 1951) has tried to establish whether given communication networks facilitate or hinder the performance of a group of four or five people in the completion of a task. These researches showed that for simple tasks basically involving the assembly of information held by different members of the group, the networks with a *central* person (wheel, Y and chain in Figure 5) proved most

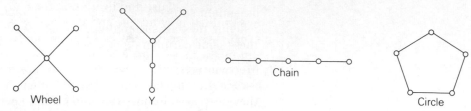

Figure 5   Five-person network

Figure 6   All-channel four person network

effective (in that order). For the solution of complex problems, the more diffuse networks of the circle groups proved faster and the all-channel communication network (Davis and Hornseth, 1967), reproduced in Figure 6, proved most effective (and superior to individuals solving the same problems on their own). It is likely that the all-channel network's superiority was due to its openness and flexibility which enabled some members to play a more prominent part and to by-pass others who were less able to cope with the task at hand. By contrast, the extent to which alternative structures can emerge in a wheel network is minimal.

central role These studies are mentioned here in our review of leadership because they provided some interesting findings concerning the central role. Those people who *by chance* held central positions in the network tended to evolve as decision-makers and were generally judged to be leaders by the other group members. In comparison with people in peripheral positions they tended to send more messages, to solve problems more quickly, to make fewer errors and to be more satisfied with group and personal efforts. In other words, it would appear that it was primarily the position in the network and not 'personality' which led to the assumption of the leadership role.

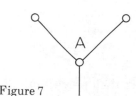

Figure 7
Four-person Y network

Berkowitz (1956) took these studies further in order to examine the interaction between personality characteristics and the central role. He used problems which had also been used by other experimenters and a Y network composed of four people with A in the central position (Figure 7): see Box 9.

In other words – if one can generalize from a laboratory experiment to the 'real' world – people can come to respond to the demands of a situation and, in the present case, behave like leaders even though, initially, they did not appear to have the psychological attributes ('high ascendancy') of a leader. This does not, of course, necessarily imply that *any* person can fill *any* role but that the demand characteristics of the role may elicit hidden talents.

More generally, these studies suggest that for simple or routine problems and decisions an explicit communication structure with a central person (such as a charge-hand or supervisor in an industrial organization) is likely to be effective. For creative or complex problems (such as may be faced by more senior management) the more open networks seem to give better results in terms of the quality of the solutions produced and in terms of personal satisfaction.

Box 9 Personality and behaviour in central and peripheral roles (Berkowitz, 1956)

In advance of the problem-solving sessions Berkowitz tested his subjects for certain personality characteristics which he designated as 'high-ascendant', 'low-ascendant' and 'moderately-ascendant'.

In half his experimental groups a high-ascendant person occupied the central position, in the other half a low-ascendant person occupied the central position. The resulting messages were coded as 'relaying' information received from others (passive behaviour) or as 'initiating' communications such as proposing solutions or asking for further information (active behaviour).

The results indicated that both personality and role requirements influenced behaviour. For instance, in the *peripheral* positions, the low-ascendant subjects sent a significantly higher percentage of information-relaying messages than did the high-ascendant subjects when occupying these same peripheral positions.

More interesting, however, is the *change* in the behaviour of low-ascendant subjects when they occupied the central positions. Over time they decreased in passivity and came to behave like high-ascendant subjects in the central position.

These studies all show the importance of having relevant information in order to arrive at the solution of problems. It is perhaps not entirely accidental, therefore, that many relatively lowly placed executives or supervisors can often be seen to display a marked tendency to hoard such information as they have and keep it from others so that those who work with them have to appeal to them for advice, guidance, instructions or decisions. Such leaders tend to cling to their central positions and may be very autocratic in their relationships. The networks of more democratic leaders are more likely to be of the all-channel variety.

2.2.6 Conclusions to section 2.2 on leadership

How does our exploration of leadership link to the topics discussed in section 1? There, in studying interactions of people and putting forward explanations of the social influence processes at work in groups, I have not referred to leadership as the authors I reviewed have not done so either. In that earlier section we were concerned mainly with spontaneously occurring influence processes between individuals or between minorities and majorities, albeit in settings created by the experimenter who could be equated with the leader. In particular, you may think that the experimenter described as an 'authority figure' by Milgram (section 1.4) corresponds to our notion of a leader: he had, at any rate in the eyes of his subjects, power and status and he exerted influence on the subjects the extent of which varied according to the conditions of each experiment. You can also think back to the discussion in section 1.6 of the notion of 'behavioural style' put forward by Moscovici and his co-workers. Consistency, investment and autonomy which were mentioned there as essential characteristics of a minority intent on influencing a majority may well also denote a leadership style.

The notion of leadership has also been referred to in Block 5. There the concept of the 'opinion leader' was introduced. As you may remember, opinion leaders were there described as informal leaders who mediate information from the media to those who look up to them as 'opinion leaders' in a particular field of knowledge, be that politics, fashion, medical innovation or anything else. They are leaders and have influence not by virtue of their formal position, authority or power but by virtue of their perceived expertise and trustworthiness. Thus, leaders may have influence without a formal platform and, conversely, formal 'leaders' can be without influence if their 'followers' turn elsewhere for guidance or the satisfaction of their needs.

The prestige of the leaders and hence the extent of their influence is something which does not derive solely or even mainly from their formal position; it is something which accrues to them over time. Once they have gained the trust and respect of those they interact with they can, and are sometimes expected to, deviate from the norms of the group. Leaders have, as Hollander (1958) termed it, acquired 'idiosyncrasy credit' and this enables them to innovate and move the group towards decisions or innovations which might not previously have been acceptable to its members. In fact, the leader becomes a minority and, where a leader is concerned with changing people, as in Lewin's discussion groups, she or he is at the outset always in a minority.

idiosyncrasy credit

In section 1.6 we discussed the influence a minority may have on the majority in a group. Are Moscovici's ideas and findings concerning the importance of the behavioural style of the minority compatible with Hollander's view? Both Moscovici and Hollander agree that a minority can influence those in the majority but they differ in explaining how such influence is achieved. Hollander proposes that a group member holding a minority position must conform initially to the majority position and prove himself competent before being allowed by others in the group to deviate and innovate without losing his influence. By contrast Moscovici and Faucheux (1972) suggest that the minority must consistently and resolutely *not* conform from the outset and that the minority's behavioural style is the source of its influence. Bray *et al.* (1982) were intrigued by these discrepancies between the two models and set up two experiments to see whether they could obtain evidence which would allow them to decide which of these models of minority influence is better supported, see Box 10.

Box 10   Social influence by group members with minority opinions: comparison of the work of Hollander and Moscovici (Bray *et al.*, 1982)

In their first experiment four-man groups discussed three opinion issues that were selected to permit a confederate to argue for the minority position. In the Hollander strategy the confederate argued the minority position only on the last issue, whereas in the Moscovici stategy he argued it on every issue. The second experiment followed the same procedure except that both male and female subjects were tested and groups contained six members with two confederates.

Bray and his colleagues found that both the Hollander and Moscovici models were supported in that the opinions of subjects were influenced significantly when compared to those of control individuals who did not receive any influence attempt. However, the Hollander model produced influence with only one person deviating from the majority, while the Moscovici model required a minority of at least two people. There were also sex differences: with male subjects, Hollander's model produced significantly greater influence than Moscovici's model; for female groups, whilst overall they were less influenced than the male groups, both models achieved similar degrees of influence.

We may conclude that Hollander's model supports the notion of the innovating leader (from which starting-point it has been derived) whilst Moscovici's model demonstrates the effect of a minority (of more than one person). In other words, the influence processes between a group and its established leader, even though she or he has begun to deviate from group norms and in that sense has become a minority, seem to be different from those which operate between a small minority and a larger majority.

ACTIVITY 7

Think yourself, first, into the position of a leader – a head-teacher or a manager or supervisor. What lessons can you draw from this Block so far which would help you in making and carrying out decisions?

Then think yourself into the position of someone who wants to resist being influenced by a leader or other group members. What lessons can you draw in that capacity from this Block?

2.3 Coercion: manipulating group membership

In order to pursue this section's theme of group membership and social control we now broaden our focus from a consideration of influence processes within groups to looking at groups in their physical and social contexts. Thus, I shall discuss here studies which focus on attempts to change the thoughts, feelings or actions of people by changing the *social or physical situation* in which they find themselves or into which they were deliberately put on the assumption that *increased control* over them was thus possible. The question which underlies our exploration in this section is whether this increased control will generate such pressures on us that we cannot maintain our opinions, beliefs and values, in other words, that we may all have a 'breaking point'. Such efforts at control are usually **coercion** referred to as coercion. Coercion tends to suggest the application of force or pressure and hence may be distinguished from more benign influence processes such as education and, perhaps, persuasion which are seen as appealing to reason, argument and logic. However, there is no universally agreed vocabulary to refer to different degrees and methods of influence and all such terms carry implicit value judgements. For instance, in this country we tend to use the word propaganda when the communicator's intentions are suspect and we doubt the veracity of the information given. In other places and times the word projects a different image. Thus, in the seventeenth century the word was used by the Catholic Church to denote its explicit policy of bringing Christianity to non-Christian countries and peoples and such propaganda was considered to be in the interests of the recipients. Education, of course, can also be considered as propaganda in that, whilst it is intended to appeal to reason and to be based on truth, it often simply conveys conventional values or skills without questioning them. For instance, in dealing with the calculation of rents or interest, neither the teacher in teaching nor the child in learning tend to reflect that they are dealing with concepts peculiar to capitalism. We are, of course, all aware of the efforts being made at present to counteract existing biases (or propaganda) in the portrayal of sex roles. Such efforts at change may however have some unintended consequences. Thus, I think, the tortured English which crops up in this Block from time to time is due to the course team's wish to avoid 'sexist' language in the use of pronouns. It is also difficult at present to find a children's book in which a little girl makes cakes or is otherwise employed in household tasks though recently I found several such books which portray boys in this way.

If it is not possible to make crystal clear distinctions between words denoting degrees of influence one can nevertheless attempt to order such words along a dimension of social acceptability, starting (probably) with socialization, education, and persuasion at the 'acceptable' end of the continuum through such processes as propaganda, manipulation and indoctrination to the extremes of coercion, brainwashing and torture.

In discussing such influence processes, however, we are not only concerned with their acceptability but also with their effectiveness. Thus, in Blocks 1 and 2 we explored the social processes resulting in the socialization of the young child; in Block 5 we considered the influences on people which affect their voting behaviour and the formation or change of attitudes. Here, in considering coercion, we may all agree that it is unethical but we need to consider in what kinds of contexts it is likely to have effects, if only so that we can learn to guard against them. The possibility of manipulating the environment in one way or another to achieve a variety of aims, good or evil, increases the control which change-agents have over those they wish to influence.

We have already seen that individuals relate to each other in manifold ways within groups and that people in groups (for instance, in Lewin's discussion groups) can be influenced more readily than when the same message is addressed to individuals (for instance, those listening to a lecture). In considering coercion we will, therefore, explore not just effects on individuals through, for example, attempts at indoctrination but, explicitly, *how group membership has been manipulated to achieve such effects.*

It is still an open question in the social sciences to what extent people do what they do because they act in accordance with their own deeply-held values or whether their behaviour is significantly influenced by the social situations in which they find themselves. The question cannot easily be resolved since most people, after all, associate with others with whom they have something in common and often choose the situations in which they find themselves. Hence their behaviour may be in accordance with their deeply-held values *and* be appropriate to their situation. However, when the social context is deliberately changed, as it was in Milgram's experiment on obedience, we may be able to explore whether changes follow in people's attitudes and behaviour.

The environment can be manipulated to have effects generally thought to be beneficial. The layout of a housing estate, for instance, may be planned to enable greater social contacts among the residents (Gans, 1972) or to reduce vandalism (Newman, 1972). Similarly the design of a psychiatric ward (Osmond, 1957) may aid interaction among patients and staff and reduce isolation and loneliness. Or, as Deutsch and Collins (1951) and others have shown, enabling black and white residents on a housing estate to make contact with each other may lead to a reduction in racial prejudice. The 'busing' of children to schools in other areas is also intended to reduce racial antagonisms (though this measure has led to other problems such as children having no friends in their own locality and it has been largely abandoned). Such manipulations of the environment, however, tend to affect only some aspects of everyday life. Here, however, we will consider the more overwhelming effects of more pervasive environmental control.

Set reading

You may like to read now, or later when we discuss intergroup relations, chapter 2 in your Course Reader (Murphy, John and Brown, 1984). This chapter, 'The perilous path: from social research to social intervention', deals with the school desegregation debate in the United States and its prime objective is to serve as an example of the difficulties social scientists face when they attempt to influence policy decisions by their expert testimony. However, this case history also illustrates the anticipated and the realized effects of changes in the social context of black and white school children and hence it may stimulate you at this juncture to think in terms of deliberately introduced environmental changes.

2.3.1 Total institutions

total institutions Total institutions have been defined by Goffman, who coined the word, 'as a place of residence and work where a large number of like-situated individuals, cut off from the wider society for an appreciable period of time, together lead an enclosed, formally administered round of life' (Goffman, 1968, p. 11). Normally, people tend to sleep, play and work in different places and with different co-participants. The central feature of total institutions can be described as a breakdown of the barriers ordinarily separating these three spheres of life. *Inmates* of total institutions (such as officer cadets, nuns, public school boys, prisoners or patients in mental hospitals) typically have only restricted contact with the world outside; the *staff* may be socially integrated with their wider society but the extent to which they may be so integrated and hence influenced by the *mores* and values of the community outside their institution may depend on their geographical situation on the one hand and, on the other, on how far they feel that outsiders understand and are sympathetic to their professional roles and responsibilities.

A total institution affords the possibility of a high level of psychological control over its inmates since the institution controls their stimulation, their response opportunities and the rewards they receive. The inmates lack access to outside contacts, roles or reference groups. However, the fact that total institutions encompass all aspects of a person's life need not in itself lead to autocratic or coercive behaviour on the part of the staff. A total institution such as a *kibbutz* or commune may be egalitarian and democratic and yet, because of the relative lack of outside contacts, may achieve great similarity in views and behaviour among its members. Whether membership is voluntary or involuntary need not be crucial to the effect of the influence of the staff (or existing members) on new entrants. According to Goffman, it is the emphasis on and institutional arrangement made for creating and maintaining *inequality* and *social distance* between inmates and staff which is the basis of the coercive power of the staff. This power can be used to rob individuals of normal supports to their conceptions of their own selves.

On admission patients are stripped of their 'identity kit' in that they may not be allowed to retain their personal possessions, wear their own clothes or even keep their own dentures. They may be referred to by a number rather than by name (and in Nazi concentration camps have this number stencilled permanently on the wrist). The inmates, according to Goffman, may be systematically degraded and mortified through the conditions of their physical environment as well as through the behaviour of the staff and they may be deprived not only of freedom but of all discretion in structuring their daily life – when to eat, sleep, go to the lavatory, or what to work at, or what activities to engage in apart from work. In these circumstances it is, according to Goffman, well nigh impossible for the inmate to maintain her or his previous self since the self, the individual's personality, is a 'persona' or mask donned for a particular audience and the result of the interaction of a performance with a specific audience: 'A correctly staged and performed scene leads the audience to impute a self to a performed character, but this imputation – the self – is a product of a scene that comes off, it is not a cause of it' (Goffman, 1971, p. 245).

This description of the self as a transient enactment of a role is, of course, not universally accepted. Goffman, however, declares that robbing people of the props to their identity is indeed to rob them of their identity. He envisages the ensuing restructuring of the self or identity as if this new self were an artificial graft, unrelated to the individual's previous personality and he declares that 'the self is not a property of the person to whom it is attributed, but dwells rather in the pattern of social control' and that the 'institutional arrangement does not so much support the self as constitute it' (Goffman, 1968, p. 154). If the latter statement were taken to be literally true then one would not expect patients to adapt in individual and diverse ways to the demands of the social structure in which they find themselves. Goffman himself describes in one of the essays ('The underlife of a public institution') in his book *Asylums* (1968) 'ways of making out in a mental hospital'. Some patients, he claims, withdraw from the situation into themselves, others make the institution their home to the extent that they do not wish to leave it and yet others become converts to the views the staff have of them. Such variations in the perception of and response to the same demands can only be explained in terms of the individual's personality, albeit diminished and robbed of its customary supports as it may be in particular institutional contexts.

Whilst one may not wish wholly to accept Goffman's sociological version of personality, one has to recognize his importance in pointing to situationally determined changes in personality or behaviour. He states quite explicitly that hospitalization (or admission to prison or some other total institution) is such a traumatic event and entails such a fundamental change in a patient's life that the effect of these changes can be studied by assuming that all patients, irrespective of symptoms or diagnosis, are faced by similar circumstances and react to them in similar ways. He writes:

> It is a tribute to the power of social forces that the uniform status of mental patients cannot only assure an aggregate of persons a common fate and eventually, because of this, a common character, but this social reworking can be done upon what is perhaps the most obstinate diversity of human materials that can be brought together by society.

(Goffman, 1968, p. 121).

One must not lose sight of the fact that the staff, too, are affected by those with whom they are in contact. They are being socialized into their roles by explicit instruction as well as by the example set by the other staff. But one may well wonder how far the agents of control are themselves controlled by their inferiors: a prison warder, say, to have a quiet life needs to reach a *modus vivendi* with her or his charges. Goffman's notions of the environment *determining* behaviour or personality echoes the old version of child socialization as a one-way influence process – a model we have explicitly rejected in Blocks 1 and 2.

Goffman, then, by taking situational variables as his only significant influences on personality and behaviour takes an extreme stand I do not share. But his views on total institutions and on personality serve as a strident and dramatic lead-in to the discussion of other coercive situations.

2.3.2   Thought reform

thought reform   The term thought reform is a translation of the Chinese word which describes the psychological techniques used by the Chinese communists to effect changes in political views and in self-concept. These techniques are also sometimes referred to as brainwashing but this seems an emotive as well as a meaningless term if it is intended to imply that the human mind can be wiped clean like a slate and a new start be made. I should like to discuss three examples of Chinese thought reform programmes as they were applied to United Nations prisoners of war in Korea, to Chinese intellectuals and to Western civilians living in China. I am focusing on these Chinese attempts at persuasion and coercion for several reasons:

(a)   because of the historical importance of these events;

(b)   because the techniques employed by the Chinese are of very great interest to psychologists and have stimulated considerable research in the United States, Britain and elsewhere; and

(c)   because we can find parallels with various techniques used by past and present religious groups.

Thought reform dates back to the early days of the Chinese communist movement (the late 1920s) when a scheme of education and propaganda was founded designed to modify 'the whole human being by giving him a totally new view of the world and awakening in him a range of feelings, reactions, thoughts, and attitudes entirely different from those to which he was accustomed' (Ellul, 1965, p. 304). Such education was directed towards the civilian population in areas under communist control and to captured soldiers. The techniques, described in the following sections, were evolved over a period of time. In so far as they were applied to their own nationals they were designed to integrate individuals into a new political order as firmly as possible and to detach them from their former groups by weakening their strong family ties and by removing them from their traditional village organizations.

Since the establishment of a Communist government in the whole of mainland China in 1949, a curious blend of continuous education and reform, together with purges of dissidents, has been developed. Ellul (1965) suggests that there have been three aspects of Chinese education and propaganda:

(a) the total integration of child education with propaganda;

(b) the development of the discussion system: the aim of such discussion is not to arrive at some ultimate truth but to gain acceptance of a previously defined view (see section 2.3.4);

(c) the notion that there is the need to press people again and again into the mould of the perfect socialist and to ensure absolute conformity of the individual to Marxist doctrine and the new structure of society (and hence, perhaps, the emphasis on reciting quotes from Mao during his chairmanship).

There are those – such as Marxist sociologists – who would say that the first point above is true of most education systems but not necessarily formally acknowledged. In other words, there may be a 'hidden curriculum', as in my earlier example of learning to calculate rent or interest.

2.3.3 Attempts at political indoctrination: prisoners of war of the Chinese during the Korean war

Chronologically, the experiences of the United Nations prisoners of war of the Chinese in the early 1950s came later than the indoctrination or re-education of Chinese intellectuals described in the next section. I am, however, starting our discussion with the experiences of these soldiers as they rekindled the interest of Western psychologists, psychiatrists and others in the study of deliberate and systematic attempts at persuasion, as has already been pointed out in Block 5. Also, the techniques used on these prisoners were not so extreme as those described in the next section. What had agitated various Western governments **mass indoctrination** and army authorities at the time was the Chinese attempt at mass indoctrination of prisoners of war during the Korean conflict. The Chinese were not merely containing men, as is usual with prisoners of war, so that they could not continue to fight on their own side: the Chinese tried to convert them to their own view of the world. Looking back now to the era of the Korean War it may strike us that the Chinese did not have a particularly startling success rate in subverting their prisoners and that the American and British overreacted to these events. We must remember, however, that in the 1950s (the period of the Cold War) many people in the West had an unshakeable belief in democracy and the virtues of the capitalist system which were seen as going hand in hand. Today, we may no longer be so self-confident about our own way of life. In the late 1960s we witnessed the disillusion of many of the younger generation in Western society. In this changed climate we may be less certain of our own values and, hence, perhaps less surprise and consternation would be caused by an attack on our values.

The conditions and experiences of prisoners of war of that period are of particular interest to *social* psychologists since such success as the Chinese had, depended on their ability to undermine the prisoners' normal social relationships in the camps and through the withholding of mail and news from home. These prisoners of war were surprised that they were expected to think of themselves as students of politics under the tutelage of their communist guards. They soon learned that their treatment as prisoners of war depended on how far their political convictions pleased their captors. 'Reactionaries' were severely punished.

At the time it was considered disturbing, surprising and incomprehensible that a considerable percentage of American prisoners of war collaborated with the enemy (Schein, 1957; Kinkead, 1959). The extent of collaboration varied from writing anti-American propaganda and informing on comrades to less serious offences such as broadcasting Christmas greetings to families at home (and hence putting the Chinese, by implication, in a favourable light). In addition, twenty-one Americans (out of some 4000 survivors) elected not to return to the United States at the end of the war (though most did so eventually). Only one British soldier out of nearly 1000 prisoners did not return home. How did the Chinese set about achieving their aims?

First of all, from a psychological point of view, the American, British and other soldiers were ill-prepared and not clearly aware of what they were fighting for. Their Chinese captors surprised them by being, initially, friendly and lenient and willing to treat the prisoners as 'students' to whom they could teach the 'truth' about the war. They explained that the United Nations had entered the war illegally and that prisoners could be shot as war criminals unless they learned what the Chinese wished them to learn, 'namely: that the Communists had a monopoly of truth; that the prisoners accepted that they had been dupes of their capitalist rulers; that they were willing to learn the "truth"; and that they welcomed their "liberation" by the Chinese' (Ministry of Defence, 1955).

Our discussion of total institutions has shown us that people have great difficulty in maintaining their views, their integrity as individuals or their normal behaviour if their social environment is designed to strip them of customary supports and reinforcement to their 'normal' selves. The Chinese, too, aimed at the total control of the prisoners' environment and social milieu. They systematically destroyed the prisoners' formal and informal *group structure*. They put their own men in charge of platoons and companies. They undermined accepted loyalties and discipline by prohibiting distinctions of rank, punishing any officer or NCO who attempted to give an order and encouraged the humiliation of officers. Eventually officers and NCOs were removed to separate camps as 'reactionaries'. The Chinese also tried to undermine informal groupings and relationships by setting men against each other. For example, if during compulsory indoctrination[2] classes (often lasting as long as eight hours at a stretch) a prisoner was recalcitrant the whole group would be made to stand until the prisoner withdrew his remarks or question. After hours of standing the prisoner's comrades would urge him to abandon his objections and he usually gave in under moral pressure from his own side. He was made to apologize and his comrades were made to criticize him. From criticism to 'informing' is a relatively small step and the Chinese managed to establish a system of informers so that the men felt they could trust no one. Interrogation often lasting for days was another technique for manipulating the prisoners – a technique only partly intended to elicit useful information. Its main purpose was to undermine the prisoners' trust in each other by the pretence that information had already been obtained from others in the camp. Thus, a person who resisted answering questions, despite great fatigue and the continued repetition of the same question, would see that he had resisted in vain when the interrogator pulled out a notebook and read the answer to him, an answer he had obtained elsewhere or had invented. The process would be repeated with a new question till eventually that person felt it was useless to resist further and to suffer in vain. Interrogation was also designed to undermine a person's self-respect since a prisoner of war is not supposed to reveal anything other than his name, rank and number. Once he had given some information, even information he knew the Chinese had already, they could increase their pressures on him to collaborate further by threatening to expose him to his comrades.

Indoctrination sessions during which intensive pressures were brought to bear on single individuals were increasingly practised by the Chinese as the war continued. They proved to be more effective than mass lectures, involving as they did a personal relationship between prisoner and instructor. Not only does a person have to listen (rather than doodle or doze as he might do at a mass meeting) when the argument is directed at him personally, but, as is often the case, his own ability to argue back is limited and he is, therefore, more vulnerable to influence even if, initially, he thinks the argument faulty or specious. In *group indoctrination* classes if no one is swayed, resistance is easier and the Chinese could be made to look foolish when they did not understand slang and idiom sufficiently to appreciate when they were being subtly ridiculed.

The obstruction of communication with home was another means of manipulating and influencing the prisoners. Usually only mail which carried bad news was delivered. The withholding of other letters increased feelings of isolation and insecurity. Parcels, books and magazines were not delivered. Only communist newspapers were available. Men were urged to communicate with relations and friends by making broadcasts which were to include peace 'propaganda'. The Chinese also appreciated that the natural longing of their captives for peace (and hence repatriation) could be channelled into forming 'peace committees' and into making apparently spontaneous appeals which might have a greater impact in the free world than overtly Chinese-originated 'propaganda'.

It must not be forgotten that psychological pressures or inducements to 'progressive' prisoners of war were backed by 'physical coercion and torture, revolting to the humane mind' (Ministry of Defence, 1955). This report gives full details of tortures reported by repatriated British prisoners of war and, independently, American soldiers reported similar tortures (Schein, 1956). Thus, in addition to beatings and imprisonment in tiny cages which were too small to sit, stand or lie in, prisoners were made to stand semi-naked and barefoot on the frozen Yalu river where water which froze immediately was poured over their feet; prisoners were left for hours with their feet frozen into the ice to reflect on their 'crimes'. Another form of torture was to fix a hangman's noose round a prisoner's neck; he was then hoisted up on his toes and the rope fixed so that if he slipped or bent his knees he would hang himself.

To what extent were these pressures and manipulations effective in producing acts of collaboration (broadcasting for the enemy, admitting to participating in germ warfare, informing on other prisoners and so on) or in producing changes in attitudes or beliefs?

Firstly, collaboration. It would appear that between ten and fifteen per cent of the American prisoners consistently collaborated in a variety of ways with the purposes of their captors and by doing so they, of course, offended against the norms of their own society. This group included people who collaborated for opportunist reasons, such as extra food or privileges, and others who were particularly vulnerable because of their low status in their home community – they often felt they had not had a proper chance in life or else looked on themselves as failures. Still others were simply weak individuals who had initially been tricked into collaboration.

A similar percentage (ten to fifteen per cent) of prisoners did not collaborate at all. They were either those who rebelled consistently against authority – when in the army or when in the situation of prisoners. Others were mature, well-integrated people with a strong sense of personal honour who could withstand the disruption of their normal social organization and support. Others, possibly, denied their strong desire to collaborate by 'reaction formation', that is, the unconscious suppression of this desire in favour of the opposite, strong resistance.

The vast majority of the prisoners, however, 'played it cool', engaging in a certain degree of overt compliance and making minor concessions such as feigning an interest in the indoctrination programme but primarily remaining passive and withdrawn. It would appear from the official British investigation (Ministry of Defence, 1955) that a somewhat smaller percentage of British prisoners collaborated with their Chinese captors. Remarkable also is the record of the Turkish prisoners. A shocking thirty-eight per cent of American prisoners had died during captivity. Whilst the living conditions were very inadequate, survival also depends on psychological factors – on 'morale'. None of the Turkish prisoners succumbed because sick and wounded prisoners were supported by their comrades. No Turkish prisoners collaborated. This has been attributed

(Kinkead, 1959) to the authoritarian attitudes of the Turks which led to their recognizing only their own superiors as valid sources of information and authority. The American army authorities were greatly disturbed by the lack of morale among those of their soldiers who were taken prisoner and they subsequently developed a new code of behaviour for American soldiers so as to increase their ability to stand their ground mentally and morally as well as physically.

Secondly, what about beliefs? Were many prisoners converted to communism? We have already mentioned that only very few prisoners refused repatriation and some of these may not have been converts to communism but were afraid of facing charges on their return home. Of those who returned one cannot know how many became newly sympathetic to communist views, how many became strengthened in the tentative views they held prior to their imprisonment, or in how many a more critical attitude to their own society was created. The important question of how likely it is that prisoners, once returned to their own society, will maintain any new-found beliefs will be discussed in section 2.3.5. One point, however, can be raised here. The extent to which the Chinese succeeded in making prisoners collaborate with them was, initially, received with a great deal of shock and surprise, largely because the military, the ordinary public and, to some extent, psychologists too, think of the person as a recognizable individual, wholly her- or himself and behaving in a fairly consistent manner. The fact that collaboration with the enemy (which, in the above view, might be considered inconsistent with what a soldier would do 'normally') took place on an unexpected scale was then explained by Schein (1956, 1957) and others, as being due, in part, to the special vulnerability or susceptibilities of some individuals; in larger measure, however, the effects were seen as being due to the control of the total 'milieu' by the Chinese which involved the prisoners in quite unexpected and not previously experienced pressures and harassment.

None of us should be so lacking in humility as to predict how we would ourselves be able to stand up to such pressures or, for that matter, how we would respond to the more transient pressures of a religious revivalist meeting. Thus, for instance, many people made a 'decision for Christ' when at a Billy Graham meeting in the 1960s, probably without a long-lasting change in beliefs or behaviour. And, as we have seen in the experiments conducted by Milgram (1974b), a high proportion of the subjects could not withstand the short-term psychological pressures created by the experimenter urging them to follow his instructions (though fewer succumbed to his influence when they were with others who were seen to disobey the experimenter). In consequence, they behaved in ways they would not 'normally' engage in, nor had various groups of experts, such as psychiatrists, expected them to act in such ways. Similarly, even the adoption of a temporary role for payment as prison guard or prisoner in an experiment (Zimbardo *et al.*, 1973) can lead to extraordinary changes in the role-players' perceptions of others and in their behaviour and attitudes towards them. (This study will be further discussed in section 2.3.6.)

By contrast, the United Nations prisoners of the Chinese and North Koreans endured their conditions of harrassment, torture and control for several years. In essence, a prisoner had several problems: how to remain alive, how to improve his living conditions, how to maintain a consistent outlook on life under conditions where basic values and beliefs were strongly undermined, and how to maintain friendship ties and concern for others under the conditions of mutual distrust, lack of leadership and social disorganization which the Chinese had created. Whilst their conditions were more extreme, the pressures and procedures they experienced are remarkably like those Goffman describes as occurring in mental hospitals where the patient, too, has to accept the description of 'reality' offered by the staff in order to ameliorate his conditions.

Was the Chinese indoctrination campaign effective? Certainly, their techniques and behaviour created conditions in which only collaboration and acceptance of communist ideologies led to resolution of the problems the prisoners faced. As we have seen, the majority of prisoners collaborated in various ways from time to time but it would appear that the Chinese were less successful in changing beliefs and values, though the indoctrination programme is likely to have had some effect at the time and later on back home, as has already been pointed out in Unit 17/18.

At this point you may wish to speculate whether the 'forced compliance' paradigm discussed in Unit 16 can be used to explain the limited success of the Chinese programme. The phrase 'forced compliance', as you may recall, refers to situations in which people feel compelled to behave in ways which do not accord with their beliefs, attitudes or feelings. They then cope with the dissonance aroused by this discrepancy by bringing their cognitions into line with their earlier behaviour. However, the more pressure people experience (from financial inducements, for instance) the less dissonance is aroused as the pressure excuses or justifies their behaviours.

Given that this paradigm has been evolved in different circumstances, it is gratifying to see that it fits the situation the prisioners were in and does not contradict the findings here. Nevertheless, one is always on dangerous ground if one uses an explanation based on temporary and uninvolving laboratory situations to explain much more pervasive, long-lasting and harrowing events. The argument I have presented in this section is more complex in that such changes in attitudes and beliefs as occurred, in the short- and long-term, were attributed to a chain of events, viz. the 'stripping' process (including the loss of support from a stable group) people need to undergo before they can be induced to adopt new beliefs.

2.3.4 Chinese revolutionary colleges and re-education

In this section I am going to discuss methods of 'thought reform' which have much in common with the psychological manipulations reviewed in the last section but go beyond them in their scope and effects.

These more intensive techniques were intended to 'retrieve' rather than to eliminate those citizens who were defined as holding erroneous political views. They were applied by the Chinese primarily to members of their own society, particularly intellectuals. Our main source of information on these 're-education' programmes is the work of Dr R. J. Lifton who in 1954 and 1955 studied some of the failures of the processes of 'thought reform'. He interviewed, in Hong Kong, twenty-five Westerners and fifteen Chinese intellectuals who had been expelled from mainland China or who had fled from there. 'Thought reform' as practised by the Chinese is interesting from a psychological point of view because it goes beyond normal processes of influence or persuasion such as social pressure, exhortation or ethical appeals. It is the extraordinary, 'combination of external force or coercion with an appeal to inner enthusiasm through evangelistic exhortation which gave thought reform its emotional scope and power' (Lifton, 1961, p. 13).

Lifton (1957) discusses the 'revolutionary colleges' set up all over China in the late 1940s and the techniques developed there for reforming the political views of the population. These colleges were mainly attended by Chinese intellectuals and officials; some were there as the result of thinly veiled threats but most were genuine volunteers eager to equip themselves for an important role in the new communist China. Students usually attended for approximately six months and Lifton distinguishes three stages 'which represent the successive psychological climates to which the student is exposed as he is guided along the path of his symbolic death and rebirth; the Great Togetherness, the closing in of the Milieu, and Submission and Rebirth' (Lifton, 1957, p. 7).

During the first stage the student becomes a member of a ten-person *study group* in which the participants discuss their experiences and their hatred of the old régime. These group experiences are complemented by lectures on the new ideologies and purposes. Then, after four to six weeks, a change begins to develop in the atmosphere – there is a shift in emphasis from the intellectual and ideological to the personal and emotional. Students begin to realize that *they* rather than communist doctrine are the object of study. Their views and attitudes come under scrutiny and the leader and other members of their primary membership group exert pressures on them to adopt the 'correct' views. Constant criticism of others and self-criticism leading to confessions and reform are required of the student. 'Backward' students with suspicious backgrounds or whose confessions are not keen enough in criticizing others are singled out, relentlessly criticized, threatened and publicly humiliated. No student can in these circumstances avoid feelings of fear, anxiety or conflict. All are fearful of being considered reactionary and found wanting. The last stage of this programme of thought reform is the student's final confession – a document of between five and twenty-five thousand words which is prepared over a period of weeks and which is read to the group where it is subjected to painful discussion and revision. When at last this confession is approved the student experiences great emotional relief. Confession is the symbolic submission to the régime and at the same time the person's rebirth into the communist community.

Is such thought reform effective? Obviously not in every case; as I have pointed out, Lifton interviewed students from these revolutionary colleges who had left China as dissident refugees. Nevertheless, there are many reasons for assuming that this programme did have wide-ranging effects. It is, again, the control of the students' environment (what Lifton refers to as 'milieu control') which makes the programme potentially so awesome and effective. He writes:

> ... [the student's] environment is so mobilized that it will psychologically support him only if he meets its standards, and will quickly and thoroughly undermine him when he fails to do so. More and more there is a blending of external and internal milieux, as his own attitudes and beliefs become identical with those of his outer environment.

> (Lifton, 1957, p. 13)

In addition, the student experiences the 'emotional catharsis of personal confession, the relief of saying the unsaid, of holding nothing back. He attains the rewards of self-surrender, of giving up his individual struggles, merging with an all-powerful force, and thereby sharing its strength' (Lifton, 1957, p. 18). 'Thought reform' is effective, in certain circumstances, not because students emerge intellectually convinced of the validity of new information, ideologies or dogmas but because they need, psychologically, to be members of their immediate group and wider society in order to have a meaningful existence. If these needs can only be met by adopting certain values and beliefs, many people will end up by making such values and beliefs their own. This, indeed, is the crucial lesson to be learned here in the context of our analysis of group phenomena.

Lifton has published a book (Lifton, 1961) which contains several moving accounts of the experiences of individuals and how the processes I have outlined led to their gradual adoption of the 'people's standpoint'. (I have put this book on the list of further reading which you will find at the end of the Block.)

Whilst the 'cultural revolution' has come to an end in China, it appears from newspaper reports, for instance on the advocacy and imposition of birth control, and from such sources as the series of television programmes first shown in 1984 on Channel 4 under the title *The Heart of the Dragon* that very similar methods are still used in China. Thus, for instance, one programme which portrayed the trial of a confessed thief showed how she repeatedly had to confess to her crime and, by European standards, humble herself and acknowledge her sin to society. She was sentenced to a year's 'surveillance' which, it was stated, would involve repeated confessions at her place of work and elsewhere. Control through group membership, coupled with the re-education of the individual, therefore seems still to be a preferred mechanism for achieving social cohesion in present-day China.

This process of adopting one's captors' views is something for which we have evidence from other sources as well. The process Freud described as identification (taking on someone else's values) was, in its original formulation, seen to achieve the resolution of the child's Oedipus complex through identification with the father, a feared competitor for his mother's affection. Bettelheim (1961) observed how some prisoners in German concentration camps identified with their captors, decked themselves out in bits of Nazi uniforms and adopted the views of their guards. The deprivations they had undergone had reduced them to a childlike state of dependence on their all-powerful captors. More recently it has been found that victims of hijacks or hostages in hold-ups also form relationships with their captors, and come to like them or to agree with them, even though, or precisely perhaps because, they are dependent on them (Jenkins, 1975), as are the naive subjects dependent on the experimenter or her or his collaborators in conformity and obedience experiments (see section 1.5). See Figure 8 for an

PSYCHOLOGY

Can those siege friendships last?

Some hostages released from the American Embassy in Teheran last week expressed a vague sympathy towards their Iranian captors. Their attitude must have been partly influenced by concern for those still held but psychiatrists acknowledge that a friendly relationship often develops between captors and captives. Can such a forced friendship survive? JOHN SHIRLEY reports:

WHEN an Italian restaurant manager named Giovanni Scrano emerged unshaven from his ordeal at the Spaghetti House Siege in October, 1975, he astonished almost everyone by speaking out in favour of the leader of the robbers who had held him at gun-point for six days and nights in a windowless basement room.

Scrano visited his former captor, Franklin Davies, in Brixton prison, taking gifts of fruit, cigarettes and cake; he organised a collection among his fellow hostages to buy Davies a Christmas present; and he offered to give *defence* evidence when Davies and his co-conspirators went on trial.

It was an eloquent testimony to the theory of "transference" which predicts that, if left long enough in a calm, secure environment, captors and captives will gradually relate to one another. During sieges police rely on this, believing that it increases their chances of persuading the captors to release their hostages unharmed.

The tactics have often worked and official interest in the unusual "friendships" naturally fades. So, no doubt, do most of the friendships. But last week The Sunday Times discovered that in the case of the "Spaghetti House friendship," the relationship is extraordinarily strong four years after the event.

Scrano visited Davies, on remand in jail, twice a week for nine months. After Davies was sentenced to 21 years for armed robbery and assault, the Home Office stopped the visits because Davies, as a top-security prisoner, could not see anyone he had not known before the robbery.

So they exchanged letters. Scrano arranged a bank account for Davies and paid in small regular amounts so Davies could buy cigarettes, stamps and small luxury items in jail. He sent him books at his request—on politics, revolution and black studies.

When Davies wanted to learn a language, Scrano posted him two French and German dictionaries.

In March this year Scrano went abroad. I tracked him down last week to the Pinnochio Restaurant in Monte Carlo, where he is a manager—and where he was finishing his latest weekly letter to Davies.

"We write about the daily hardships of our lives," he said. "Running a restaurant is not always easy, and being in prison is a difficult life. I tell him news about my family and he gives me advice. He says I should be careful, and be sure to be honest in my dealings with other people.

"I think he is a wonderful man. We have formed a creative and close friendship. I am his only contact with the outside world."

During the siege, says Scrano, "We realised we had much in common. We were both foreigners working in a hostile land. I am from southern Italy. In my country, that is like being a black man in England." Davies was the leader who persuaded the others to give up, says Scrano. "I hope we shall remain in contact until he is free again."

● Next Thursday. BBC1's Play for Today explores the Spaghetti House Siege.

Figure 8 Affinity between hostage and captor

Source: *Sunday Times*, 25 November 1979

example of this phenomenon which you may recall.

Patti Hearst is perhaps the most extreme and best known example of this dependence on captors which led to her adopting the role and identity of 'Tania' and apparently joining in the pursuits of the 'Symbionese Liberation Army'. In her own book (Hearst, 1983) she gives an account of her extraordinary experiences during her captivity. Incidentally, Dr Lifton whom I mentioned for his research on returning soldiers and on dissidents and refugees from China, was one of the expert defence witnesses at her trial, the implication being that her experiences paralleled those of the prisoners of war and those subjected to thought reform in Chinese revolutionary colleges.

You may recall that when the American hostages in Teheran were released in 1980 after more than a year's captivity, they were not immediately flown home to be reunited with their families but were sent to an American base in Wiesbaden, West Germany, as the American authorities feared that they would be too disorientated to cope with family relationships and that it would be necessary to provide professional help for their 're-entry' problems into normal society. In the light of what we know about captor/captives relationships we must assume that the Americans feared that their fellow citizens might have been affected in their views by their dependence on their captors.

2.3.5 Short- and long-term effects of thought reform

The methods used by the Chinese during the 1950s towards prisoners of war, their own citizens and Western civilian prisoners aroused, at the time, a great deal of anxiety and discussion. Several questions remain pertinent even now. First, are these methods quite different and more destructive of an individual's self-concept and integrity than other methods designed to influence which had been previously employed? Secondly, what are the long-term effects of mass or individual indoctrination programmes?

With regard to the first question, one can certainly say that the methods employed by the Chinese are not entirely new and their effects not mysterious. Similar psychological techniques had been used by the Russians in their 1930s show trials when Western observers were surprised to see political dissidents admit their crimes of dissent even though they did not look as if they had been beaten up or tortured. They had become convinced of their own guilt since dissent from the party line to a communist *is* a crime. But history is full of people confessing to crimes such as witchcraft which they probably did not commit and, indeed, people make statements at police stations which they later retract. It is relatively easy to disorientate a person by lack of food and sleep, lack of companionship or ignorance of the passage of time (by being kept in a permanently lit or a permanently dark room). Such disorientation makes people suggestible as well as psychologically dependent on an interrogator – their only human contact. The Chinese elaborated on such methods, particularly by their use of relentless group pressure. But is such pressure different in kind or only in degree from the influences exerted by the group over the individual as discussed in section 1?

The difference between 'normal' group processes and the manipulations described here probably rests on the lack of other contacts and information over a long period of time which eliminates choice for the individual, reality-testing or consensual validation except when she or he speaks from the 'correct' standpoint. As our brief discussion of Goffman's analysis of total institutions has shown, whether an inmate is there voluntarily or not is not the crucial factor which determines the extent to which she or he is likely to be influenced in her or his new surroundings. As we have seen, it is the 'stripping' processes which people undergo and the lack of choice in human contacts which force a new personality or, in our present context, new political views on her or him. In the mass indoctrination programme of their prisoners of war the Chinese had to attempt to undermine previous social relationships before they could hope to make an impact. The students at their revolutionary colleges, too, were placed into a social context which made it difficult to retain former views. Such relentless pressure from the social milieu, the experience of guilt and release by confession are so effective one wonders whether the torture and hardship inflicted on the prisoners of war were really necessary to achieve 're-education', though no doubt they ensured that people were trapped into acts of collaboration or into making confessions, even phony ones, which then could be used against them.

Although most of my examples have been taken from twentieth-century China, I do not wish you to think that these techniques for persuasion are peculiarly Chinese. Such techniques have been employed by religious bodies and mass movements throughout history. Thus, the Inquisition used coercion; confession, criticism and self-criticism are part of the Catholic religion, of Protestant revivalist groups and of Moral Rearmament. But it is the total control of the social milieu which is the source of the helplessness of the victim.

The methods employed by the Chinese, then, are not wholly new nor specifically Chinese. Nor are they incomprehensible in psychological terms, though they may not have previously been employed so relentlessly or on so many people. Even so, as we have seen, many people do manage to resist doing what is required of them or resist adopting new beliefs. Indeed, one may say that people resist, adapt and conform according to their own deep-seated personalities and many individuals are remarkable for the inner resources that they can call forth under extreme stress. We have already mentioned that Goffman, somewhat unexpectedly in view of his notion that personality is only a transient stance a person adopts in response to situational expectations, showed that mental patients adapt to their hospital environment in personal and idiosyncratic ways. I have mentioned that among the prisoners of war those who previously were obstreperous towards those in authority continued to resist pressures from the Chinese. Lifton (1961) in his interviews with Western civilians expelled from China also shows that each person responded to his ordeal in terms of his own personality and fundamental beliefs.

Whilst one can describe the techniques used by the Chinese in terms of Western psychological, psychiatric or theological terms perhaps one still has to ask *why* thought reform was so relentlessly pursued by them. Thought reform certainly is a means of *social* control but the emphasis in the Chinese programme has been on the reform and redemption of the *individual*, not just on repression or purges of dissidents. Their insistence on implementing these processes of thought reform might nevertheless appear destructive of human integrity, identity and dignity to an observer from another cultural tradition. There remain, then, very important ethical questions.

How can we answer our second question concerning the long-term effects of the methods used by the Chinese?

We have seen in discussing Kelman's model in section 1.5.1 that the psychological effects of group membership may persist even when the individual is no longer a member of the group. Such effects on values or behaviour persist if individuals have made the group's standards their own and, therefore, do not need the support of the group to maintain their new-found beliefs. However, people tend to adopt new views or new ways of behaving as their own only if they fit in with other important values they already hold or if they offer a way of attaining goals they have previously accepted or set for themselves.

Political indoctrination of Western prisoners of war, as we have seen, was relatively ineffective even in the short run. Acts of collaboration do not necessarily imply acceptance of new political doctrines; they may merely indicate a strategy for survival. Once a soldier returns home, even if he has adopted new views, he is unlikely to maintain his views in a society which does not support them. Some who made the new views their own, of course, did not return home but stayed in China. Even then some returned later. Nevertheless, if we can draw a parallel to the Bennington college study (in Box 2 in section 1.2) we may speculate that those who had adopted new views during their captivity might on their return have sought out like-minded people and information to support their new beliefs. The Chinese students emerging from the Chinese revolutionary colleges were in a different psychological situation. They returned to a society which upheld and supported the ideas and values they had adopted in the colleges.

In assessing the likelihood of people changing their values when subjected to intense, orchestrated pressure one must consider three interlocking aspects:

(a)   a person's initial values, attitudes and knowledge, on the one hand, and her or his personal susceptibility to succumb to pressures, on the other;

(b)   the techniques employed by the change-agent, the extremity of the situation in which the person finds her- or himself, and the length of time during which a person is isolated from contrary, outside influences;

(c)   the social situation into which the individual emerges – whether or not it is supportive of new views or behaviour he or she may have adopted.

The above three criteria apply to most situations in which change is expected of a person. Thus, less drastically, successful socialization into a professional role, or learning to be an accepted member of a school community, or equipping oneself to be an officer of one's country's armed forces all depend on the interplay of these three factors. Therefore, what I have termed 'coercion' is only an extreme version of influence processes occurring constantly around us. What makes 'coercion' different is the *extremity* of the measures employed, particularly the isolation of the individual from her or his previous group membership and the fact that it is imposed upon the person. Thus we need to distinguish between a postulant in a convent having exposed herself voluntarily to the stripping of her 'normal' supports and the prisoners of war forced into such a process, even though the psychological outcomes for both may be similar.

The desired political effects of coercive methods can be shown to be limited and dependent on antecedent personal characteristics as well as on post-treatment situational factors. Nevertheless, Lifton's work would suggest that people are unlikely to emerge unchanged from the insights they have gained through these intensive onslaughts on their thoughts and the self-questioning which it provoked. They may be stronger, having undergone extreme physical and psychological pain and come out of their experiences with some degree of self-respect. At times, however, the insights gained into repressed and previously unknown aspects of the mind may well have left them shaken and disturbed. Indeed, to a minor extent, the same could be said of Milgram's subjects who needed careful 'debriefing' to adjust to their disturbing experiences.

2.3.6   Further research

As I have explained, the psychological pressures and indoctrination programmes employed against Allied prisoners of war, whilst not unique in kind (though perhaps in scale), aroused great anxiety in the West and raised questions about the nature of loyalty and treason and the preparation of soldiers for captivity. For this reason, the returning prisoners of war were extensively studied by the military, psychologists and psychiatrists in several countries, and much research was subsequently undertaken, often financed by military authorities. For instance, Hebb (Hebb *et al.* (1952) quoted by Watson (1980)) studied the disorientating effects of sensory and sleep deprivation for the Defence Research Board in Canada and Zimbardo (1973), supported by the US Office of Naval Research, set up a fake prison to study the effects of imprisonment. From such research have been learnt lessons on how to resist indoctrination and the stresses of captivity. Some of these lessons have been incorporated into military training. Perhaps you will find the implications of Zimbardo's study (outlined in Box 11) as disturbing as the indoctrination programmes I have described.

sensory deprivation

There is no doubt that this experiment provided a very real experience for the participants. You may well think that the results are as disturbing as Milgram's findings in demonstrating how easily people can come to behave in

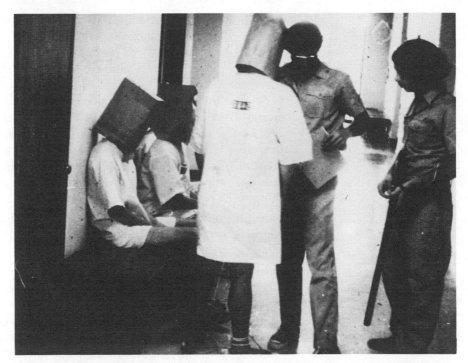
'uncharacteristic' ways when placed into new physical and social situations and are given the chance to adopt new roles, even temporarily. Both studies testify to 'the power of social, institutional forces to make good men engage in evil deeds' (Zimbardo, 1973). One finding, which is of importance in our present context, was that the prisoners did not manage to form a cohesive and supportive group; in fact they deprecated each other. The implication is that, had they managed to form such groups, they could have maintained their normal identity more successfully. One lesson to be learned, then, for life in captivity, is to form bonds with others and, rather than focus on the conditions of imprisonment, prisoners should use every opportunity to escape mentally from it. Much earlier Bettelheim (1961) who managed to survive a Nazi concentration camp found that by studying his fellow prisoners he had a purpose in life and this prevented him from succumbing to despair.

Whilst the lessons to be learnt from such post-Korean War research undoubtedly can be used to prepare people to withstand pressures in the event they are taken prisoners, the very same research, of course, also pinpoints *how* to carry out effective interrogations, *how* to disorientate prisoners and weaken their resistance and such methods, unfortunately, seem to be in use in many countries.

Recommended reading

You might (if you have not already done so) now like to read the papers by Savin (1973) and by Zimbardo (1973) in chapter 4 of the Course Reader (Murphy, John and Brown, 1984). Savin questions the ethical propriety of Zimbardo's study and Zimbardo, in reply, defends himself and underlines the lessons to be learned from this study. In chapter 5 there is also an excerpt from Watson's book *War in the Mind* (1980) on the dynamics of captivity. In addition to a description of the experiences of the prisoners of war in Korea and of Zimbardo's study which are discussed here, this excerpt also refers to German concentration camps, Japanese prisoner of war camps and the *Pueblo* incident.

ACTIVITY 8

Assuming you would like to get people to change some aspect of their behaviour – say, to reduce smoking or give it up altogether, or to adopt an innovation at work – list what you have learned from this Block which might help you to get people to change their behaviour in the desired direction.

2.3.7 Mass suicide

On 18 November 1978 over 900 people committed suicide at Jonestown in Guyana. What took place on that day caused shock and dismay in the United States and elsewhere. My reason for including this tragic and disturbing event in this section is that the accounts which have been published (amongst others: Yee and Layton, 1981; Sorrell, 1978; Naipaul, 1981; Dwyer, 1979) suggest firstly, that the techniques practised by the cult leader, the Reverend Jim Jones, closely correspond to those I have already described in the previous sections and, secondly, that one cannot begin to understand these events unless one sees them as part of a larger social scene.

Jim Jones was a self-appointed Messiah who founded the People's Temple which attracted many who wanted to escape the pressures of modern society and find new forms of spiritual experience. At the beginning, his community in San Francisco was engaged in anti-racist and humanitarian work; it was multiracial and Jones saw himself as fighting civil and religious corruption. He became paranoid about the (possibly imaginery) dangers posed to his movement by the CIA, the FBI and others and eventually transferred his community (having failed to be allowed to settle in Russia) to the jungles of Guyana to create an ideal society based on agriculture in the virgin forest. Here, even more than he had managed to do in California, he was able to isolate his followers from outside influences and to control their lives minutely. Individuals were, in addition, subjected to a barrage of propaganda and indoctrination, to forced confessions of 'crimes' and sexual activities and to physical punishments. People were also weakened through hard labour, frequent fasting, poor nutrition, lack of sleep and constant chanting of slogans. Families were broken up and divided (Yee and Layton, 1981), another instance of robbing people of customary support. Whilst we may accept that Jones was a charismatic leader[3], the extent of his control over his followers was based on the techniques he used to influence them as well as their isolation in what can only be described as a concentration camp in the jungle which was policed by armed guards. To bind his followers even more closely to him, as Hitler and others have done, he pointed to hostile groups outside the community and created the delusion that they were threatened by outsiders. As part of his cult, his followers were made to engage in repeated rehearsals of mass suicide on the grounds that suicide was preferable to the fate that might await them.

Mass suicides have historical precedents, from Masada in AD 73 where 960 Jews chose death rather than become Roman slaves, to the mass suicides of Japanese soldiers and civilians on Saipan to avoid being taken prisoner (a shameful condition for the Japanese of that period[4]) by the Americans towards the end of the Second World War. The threat to Jonestown, however, was largely imaginary, though the actual act of mass suicide was triggered off by the visit (and murder) of US Congressman Ryan who had come at the behest of anxious relatives who had been unable to get in touch with members of their families at Jonestown, and the decision of two families to use his visit to leave the community. Whilst there were no survivors at Jonestown, we have a clear picture of the events of that day as the whole macabre proceedings were tape-recorded.

Figure 10   Jonestown, Guyana: bodies lie strewn about a vat containing a drink laced with cyanide at the Jonestown commune of the People's Temple

Whilst other contemporary cults in Western society – particularly prevalent in California (see Naipaul, 1981) – have not had such tragic outcomes, it is worth noting that the Reverend Jones and his People's Temple were only one of many cults springing up at that time, all perhaps fired by the need people may have to believe in something beyond their own, maybe banal, existence and a desire for social justice and equality. It is possible that these various cults developed in response to the decline of organized religion and of parental authority and in the search for a meaningful life in a period of great social changes and disillusion. (The need for meaning is discussed in Block 4.) All such cults which have succeeded in establishing themselves have used similar techniques to disengage people from their normal contexts. Thus, for instance, the Moonies start by getting their potential followers to renounce their families and to give up their personal property: both may imply that, should they want to leave, they have nowhere to turn to and no means of escape. The next step is to fasten them to whatever beliefs are advocated by incorporating them into new group memberships, by indoctrination, confessions and public commitment.

Whilst such cults engulf only a small minority of people and are, therefore, an unusual milieu, they illustrate the fact that an individual's behaviour and experience needs to be understood in terms of her or his group memberships and the groups, in turn, must be viewed as part of the wider social structure and of current ideologies. Social movements, in general, as we shall see in Unit 22, can only be understood in terms of their own historical period.

2.4   Conclusions to section 2

In this section we have ranged very widely – from decision-making, the relationship between leaders and followers, the experiences of prisoners and hijack victims, to mass suicide and religious cults. Common to all the research and real-life material was the attempt to influence people through group membership, though the techniques employed ranged from self-persuasion to torture and coercion.

We started with Lewin (in section 2.1) who not only thought that group discussions will lead to the acceptance of new ideas or solutions but that the outcome of group discussions would be the adoption of more *rational* decisions or views. As I have pointed out, for him there was a close relationship between reason and the democratic process.

In discussing leadership (section 2.2) we again started with Lewin and his ideas on leadership style affecting the atmosphere of a group, the subjective experience of its members and the group's productivity. Exploring leadership further we saw that it could only be properly understood in the context of the needs of the group members and in the context of the wider society and its norms and ideologies.

We then moved to exploring situations in which people were taken from their normal surroundings and normal group memberships (section 2.3) – people in mental hospitals, monasteries, prisoners-of-war camps, in revolutionary colleges or in virgin forest (as members of a religious sect) and, indeed, in psychological experiments. In all these examples we saw that it is easier to disorientate an individual thus divorced from the normal supports to her or his identity. We also saw that new group memberships could be explicitly used to get the individual to adopt new views. We explored the likelihood of such indoctrination processes leading to relatively permanent changes in an individual's outlook. Implicit in our discussion is the question of how far individuals have a stable and continuing existence outside the groups which provide and support their conception of themselves. Some of the evidence I presented seems to show that there is often a personal core or self which struggles to maintain itself. Other studies, and particularly those concerned with mass suicide, would point to the supremacy of the group over the individual.

Finally, I would like you to think back to the discussion in Unit 17/18 of the counter-balancing of media influences and those arising from group membership. Indeed, as you will remember, research on mass media influences arose from the fear that people would be helpless *vis-à-vis* media influences but research, detailed in that earlier Unit, led to the 'rediscovery of the group' and of the importance of interpersonal relations in mediating information from the mass media to individuals.

Primary group membership protects the individual from unwanted and undue outside influences. But, equally, when manipulated in the way described in this section, it is a powerful tool to force new views on the individual whether this process is referred to as 'coercion' or as 're-education'.

3 INTERGROUP RELATIONS AND CONFLICTS: FROM PREJUDICE TO OUTGROUP REJECTION

In earlier sections of this Block we saw that group membership plays an important part in the life of individuals. Our main focus so far has been the psychological influences between individuals who belong to the *same* group

intragroup relations (*intragroup relations*) and the accompanying or consequent cognitive or affective
intraindividual changes changes in the individuals who form the group (*intraindividual changes*). We have seen that people can be members of, that is, psychologically relate themselves to, many different groups and we have referred to such groups, depending on the context in which we studied them, as primary groups, membership or reference groups.

intergroup relations In turning to the study of *intergroup* relations, we need to define another set of
ingroup concepts: ingroup and outgroup. Those social units of which the member feels psy-
outgroup chologically a part can be said to constitute her or his ingroups, those of which people do not feel a part and from which they wish to distinguish themselves constitute their outgroups – and one person's outgroup is, of course, another's ingroup.

The study of intergroup relations focuses on relations between small primary groups (including ephemeral laboratory groups) as well as on the relations between groups, such as national or racial groups, which have through history developed their own special cultural and social characteristics.

On the primary group level, there is some evidence (which we will explore) that the psychological satisfaction to be gained by group membership is enhanced by the existence of an outgroup, whether real or imaginary. Indeed we shall see that, at any rate in the laboratory, quite arbitrarily defined ingroups will discriminate in their distribution or rewards to equally arbitrarily defined outgroups, apparently for the sole purpose of creating and experiencing the satisfaction of ingroup membership. Outside the laboratory, too, we have ample evidence that people tend to categorize themselves as members of distinct racial or national groups or as members of distinct language, religious or ideological groups (even though they may also be part of a larger grouping such as a nation). Other ingroup/outgroup identifications may distinguish between 'labour' and 'management' or between rival groups of fans at football matches and so on.

One question we need to face in the exploration of intergroup relations concerns the origins of such self-categorizations. Are they primarily based on the need to feel part of a group and is this need satisfied by distinguishing oneself from members of other groups? This, as we shall see, is in certain circumstances an important psychological mechanism. However, it would be simple-minded in the extreme to attribute the problems of race relations or worker–management relations to purely psychological processes since such relations have a long history which includes economic or legal discrimination creating inequalities in status and in access to rewards.

labelling On a psychological level, identification with an ingroup is often created or strengthened by rejection or discrimination from outgroups (though whether a person considers this is sufficient compensation for the discrimination or persecution suffered is another question). Thus, German Jews who thought of themselves as Germans were made aware of, and began to identify with, Jewish culture and beliefs in the wake of persecution in the 1930s. The question therefore needs to be raised as to whether 'labelling' minority groups as Jews, Blacks, Catholics or whatever other categories might be available leads to people creating for themselves an identity apart from other groups where they might previously not have done so? The 'black is beautiful' slogan exactly describes this process of a stronger ingroup identification and the development of a positive self-image in the wake of hostility and discrimination from outside the group. It is quite possible that, in the absence of rejection or discrimination from others, religious or racial minorities would think of themselves as part of the larger group, such as the nation, of which they also form a part. Individuals are thus propelled into group memberships which may, previously, not have been very salient to them and it is likely that they will increasingly come to recognize these groups as relevant ingroups for themselves in a variety of contexts. In this country, many Commonwealth immigrants arrived with the idea that they were British, that they would form part of the British community, but too often they have retreated into a stronger identification with their country of origin because of the social categorizations forced on them by the host community. This is a particularly difficult problem for the children of immigrants who feel rejected, though born in England, and who do not have a strong affinity or links with the country from which their parents came. In consequence, as has been shown in Unit 6, West Indian children in Britain may adopt a dialect which strengthens their identity with the West Indies.

Identification with a group then, depends not only on the self-perceived differences between one's own group and others but also on the attitudes of members of other groups who may force an unsought-for distinction of one's own group from others by 'labelling' or other psychological processes or by the short- or long-term creation of inequalities between two groups.

The study of intergroup relations has long been a topic of interest to social psychologists, in part because intergroup relations are often fraught with conflict (and social psychologists hope to contribute to the resolution of such conflicts) and in part because it is a truly *social* psychological topic as it focuses on those relations between individuals which are determined to a considerable extent, not by their personal relationships or individual characteristics, but by their membership of different social groups. A very good example of this is the conflict between Protestants and Catholics in Northern Ireland, a conflict with a three-hundred-year tradition of hostility, the present manifestations of which cannot be attributed to hostility between individuals for personal reasons.

We shall now turn to explore the questions and issues which have been raised by social psychologists in their study of intergroup relations and conflict.

3.1 Incompatible goals

I want to start our discussions of intergroup relations and conflict between groups by drawing on another classic series of experiments which have largely stood the test of time. These studies focused on small groups of boys rather than larger social groups with a history of differences behind them. They were carried out between 1949 and 1953 by an author whose work we have already considered in section 1, Muzafer Sherif, in collaboration with his wife and other social psychologists (Sherif and Sherif, 1953; Sherif *et al.*, 1955; Sherif *et al.*, 1961). Their studies are notable not only for their findings and theoretical formulations but for the ingenuity of their methods. They used summer camps for boys of about

field experiment twelve years old as locations for realistic field experiments. The boys who participated in the experiments, however, did not know this at the time. They believed the camp to be a genuine summer camp, something very familiar to American children, and they thought the researchers were the camp staff. Now read Box 12.

Box 12   Ingroups and outgroups (Sherif and Sherif, 1953; Sherif *et al.*, 1955; Sherif *et al.*, 1961)

Sherif and his colleagues started by inviting twenty-two boys to a summer camp. The boys came from similar backgrounds but did not know each other until they met in the camp. Two separate groups were formed by allocating the boys to two different cabins. The boys engaged in the usual camp tasks and activities which required their cooperation within their own group. The purpose of the first week was to study the evolution of group norms and of a group structure in each of the groups. It was noted, not unexpectedly, that the boys in each group became friendly with each other and that a strong ingroup feeling developed. In one experiment, Sherif deliberately split up boys who had become friendly with each other within their original groups at the camp into new separate groups. Quickly, new ingroup relations were again established and within a few days they ignored previous friends and instead chose as friends members of their new groups.

In these studies, once two distinct groups had been formed, the groups were brought into contact in competitive and frustrating conditions, designed to create conflict between the two groups: specifically, matters were arranged so that the success of one group in games or other camp activities inevitably meant defeat for the other, that is, the goals of the two groups were, and were seen as, incompatible.

What were the consequences? Quite quickly *unfavourable attitudes and stereotypes* developed about the members of the *other group* and the boys did not want to have anything to do with those in the other group even though they did not differ in background and had been matched closely in physical and personal characteristics.

A second consequence was the *over-evaluation of the ingroup* and a strengthening of self-justifying attitudes towards one's own group. Cooperation increased within the group (though one group deposed its demoralized leader) and *animosity towards the outgroup* also increased. Sherif and his colleagues then explored how to reduce the hostile attitudes and behaviour of each group towards the other: see Box 13.

Through these cooperative activities, forced on the boys by the needs of the situation, hostility and unfavourable stereotypes were indeed reduced. This happened not as a result of any one event, but over a period of time during which the boys mixed more freely, became more friendly with each other and eventually travelled home peacefully in the same bus.

What conclusions can we draw from this series of experiments?

First, as we already know from earlier sections in this Block, groups are formed when people have the opportunity to interact and become interdependent.

Secondly, intergroup hostility and discrimination can be engineered through competition between two groups and such competition increases positive ingroup evaluation, rejection of the outgroup and conflict between the groups. Hostile

superordinate goals

attitudes and behaviour, in this viewpoint, are seen to _follow_ from the situation thus created, not the other way round – another instance, perhaps, of the reduction of cognitive dissonance where attitudes and beliefs are aligned with the behaviour already engaged in. But intergroup behaviour here is specifically seen not as based on the original attitudes of individuals but as 'grounded' in 'the social facts' (Durkheim, 1897) of competition or cooperation resulting from group membership. It is the incompatibility of group interests and goals which causes intergroup hostility and conflict according to this view.

Thirdly, communications and contacts between hostile groups rather than improving matters become occasions for recrimination and hostility unless superordinate goals are established which have compelling objectives for all concerned and which can only be reached by their cooperation. One might also think that 'superordinate' ideologies (such as 'what is important is playing the game, not winning') could reduce or prevent conflict. But perhaps American schoolboys have not been exposed to this particular ideology.

Fourthly, superordinate goals, in this case at any rate, lead to the dissolution of the two separate groups and the formation of a single 'superordinate' group as a result of all the boys jointly overcoming the difficulties they all faced. This is reminiscent of times of war when greater social cohesion can be achieved (though in Britain after the Second World War the class struggle re-emerged and became again a focal point in the elections of 1945). The resolution of industrial conflict, too, depends on both employers and employees recognizing the superordinate goal of their continued existence.

We can note, then, that superordinate goals, maintained over a period of time, can contribute to reducing hostility but I will postpone drawing more general conclusions from these studies till we have looked at ideas and research on other aspects of intergroup relations. Hence, we shall next turn to look at intergroup relations by taking attitudes (rather than group membership) as our starting point.

3.2 Attitudes and prejudice

Laypeople as well as social psychologists quite reasonably think that prejudice and discrimination and other hostile acts derive not only from incompatible goals or competition for scarce resources, but from hostile attitudes and, particularly, the attitudes of the members of the majority towards the minority. Attitudes and their relationship to behaviour have been extensively discussed in Block 5. You have also there explored the concept of the authoritarian personality and the interplay between society and personality, stereotyping, ethnocentrism and scapegoating. Here I would like to return to some of these issues and discuss how the attitudes associated with such a personality may influence relations with an outgroup.

authoritarian
personality

As I have pointed out at the beginning of this Block, much of the classic empirical work in social psychology was initiated and subsequently flourished in the United States. There a very natural focus of research has been the origins and manifestations of racial prejudice. In this context it can be shown that both those social attitudes which derived from prevalent social norms and ego-involved or ego-defensive attitudes adopted by the individual to safeguard a person's conception of her- or himself contribute to our understanding of prejudice (which may be defined as hostile *attitudes*) and discrimination (which refers to hostile *behaviour* towards individuals and scapegoated groups). Thus, at times, we can legitimately focus on individuals and look on their prejudices as the externalization of conflicts within the personality and, at other times, we need to look on prejudiced attitudes or overt hostility as a reflection of the behavioural norms and collective representations of a society. Now read Box 14.

Box 14　Race relations in a coalfield (Minard, 1952)

Minard (who was also mentioned in Unit 16) in a study of a West Virginian coal-mining community demonstrated the interplay of socio-cultural attitudes and individual attitudes which deviated from the prevalent social norms. The norms of this community, at that time, required segregation between black and white people. However, in the mines both racial groups had face-to-face contacts, experienced the same hardships and dangers, did the same work, and achieved the same output. In this situation friendliness and cooperation between the two groups became the social norm and Minard estimated that sixty per cent of the white miners 'integrated' below ground but continued to discriminate against their black colleagues above ground, that is, in both situations they conformed to the prevailing norms for social behaviour. About twenty per cent of the white miners segregated themselves from their black colleagues both above and below ground (that is, they did not adopt the new below-ground-integration norm) and the remaining twenty per cent attempted social integration in both situations (that is, they deviated above ground from the prevailing norms).

The minorities who did not conform to the social norms (above and below ground) may well be assumed to have had personal reasons or attributes which enabled them to resist social pressures to conform to prevailing norms. Alternatively, those who adopted new norms both below and above ground may, like Sherif's boys, be seen to have developed new attitudes as a consequence of new experiences, in this case interaction with black people on equal terms in the mines, and they carried this new norm into other relationships outside the immediate situation.

Pettigrew (1958, 1964) also demonstrated the interplay of personality and socio-cultural factors. He showed that the differences in racial attitudes between the south and the north in the United States reflected the prevailing social norms and that personality differences played only a minor role. In particular, his research showed that the more pervasive anti-black attitudes in the south were not partnered by antisemitism or authoritarianism as would be predicted by the theory of the authoritarian personality. Incidentally, we may note that research on race relations before the 1970s always explored the attitudes of white people; the attitudes of black people were ignored. To be charitable one might, of course, accept that in that earlier period it was the economically more powerful whites who were in a position to discriminate and that hence the exploration (and change) of their attitudes was more important. But it is not surprising, given that social scientists thought of black/white relations as requiring a change of attitudes among the majority population, that they were unprepared for 'a situation in which a major part of the initiative for change did not come from the white man but rather from the black' (Coser, 1967, p. 148).

In this section we have taken up the topic of attitudes once more to illustrate that the attitudes people hold may *precede* interactions between members of different groups. Attitudes hence can be looked upon as the *precursor* of intergroup behaviour – whether cooperation or discrimination; as well as that they can develop, as in the case of Sherif's boys on their camping holiday, as the *consequence* of prior interaction.

Of course, the attitudes prevalent in a particular society, or subgroup of such a society, can only be understood in terms of the history of the society or group, its economic and political experience as well as the personal experience of its members. Hence, explanations based on hostile attitudes do not exclude incompatible goals as causal factors in intergroup conflict; such explanations merely point out that attitudes and beliefs, once they exist, can become causal factors in their own right.

So far, then, we have seen that intergroup conflict can trigger off new attitudes towards the members of another group (section 3.1) *or* that the interaction may be largely determined by the prior attitudes of the members of the interacting groups (section 3.2) – whether such attitudes are non-conforming or ego-defensive or, indeed, both at the same time. In the next section, however, we shall see that intergroup discrimination may occur in the absence of prior hostile attitudes and that the mere *perception* of the existence of two groups is at times sufficient for such behaviour to occur.

3.3 The minimal group

The suggestion that the arbitrary division of people into groups is a sufficient condition for discriminatory behaviour to occur is based on the work of Tajfel and his colleagues (Tajfel *et al.*, 1971; Billig and Tajfel, 1973; Tajfel, 1978; Tajfel and Turner, 1979). They argued that before any discrimination can occur there must be a categorization of people as members of ingroups and outgroups. However, the novel point they make (and which their experiments verify) is that the very act of categorization *by itself* leads to intergroup behaviours which discriminate against the outgroup and favour the ingroup (Tajfel *et al.*, 1971). In their experiments they were able to isolate social categorization from variables such as friendship or a common purpose or task in which group members might be involved. They eliminated face-to-face contact, conflict of interests, the possibility of any previous hostility or any utilitarian or instrumental link between subjects' responses and their self-interest. What they did was to create artificial groups among fourteen- to fifteen-year-old comprehensive schoolboys in Bristol.

minimal group These 'minimal' groups which were bereft of all the features which normally characterize intergroup relations were formed on the basis of arbitrary and superficial criteria (for instance, the toss of a coin or the preference the boys expressed for the reproduction of one of two paintings), or, indeed, on a completely random basis (Billig and Tajfel, 1973) so as to eliminate the explanation that 'perceived similarity' among group members was responsible for the outcome of these experiments. Nevertheless, when individual group members, working on their own in separate cubicles, were given the opportunity of behaving in ways which would benefit other anonymous, unknown and unseen members of their own group (all they knew was that they *were* members of their own group) to the detriment of the members of the *other* group – by awarding more points or other rewards to members of their 'own' group – this opportunity was frequently taken. This was so even when in some of the experiments a non-discriminatory or cooperative strategy would have maximized the outcome for ingroup members. There was evidently a desire to maximize the *differentials* between the groups (the better to set each group apart from the other) even when there was no other reason for competitiveness.

Setting oneself off against others is quite a common experience in life. Thus, if you are a wage or salary earner, your satisfaction with the level of your remuneration may derive, at least in part, not from its absolute amount but from the differentials established between your income and that of those who earn less. You may be able to justify your view that a person of your skill or educational level or experience should earn more than those with less education, training or experience (though such justifications can be argued against) but in the 'minimal group' experiments there was no meaningful criterion for setting oneself off against others except the arbitrary division into groups. We are faced here with experimenter-created definitions of the situation where the subjects have no opportunity to examine the basis of the division or to gain information on the members of their own group or of those of the outgroup. However, the fact that the subjects are given only minimal information – mere categorization – does not invalidate the findings; on the contrary, it makes them all the more startling and thought-provoking (though the very artificiality of the situation requires caution in extrapolating from these experiments to other situations). *If* ingroup membership had not mattered to these boys, they would have allocated points and rewards at random (although once they started by rewarding ingroup members, **response norm** this might have been the beginning of a 'response norm' as we noted in discussing experiments using the autokinetic effect (section 1.1)).

What psychological processes are likely to be at work here? Tajfel and Turner state: 'Two points stand out: first, minimal intergroup discrimination is not based on incompatible group interests; second, the baseline conditions for intergroup competition seem indeed so minimal as to cause the suspicions that we are dealing here with some factor or process inherent in the intergroup situations itself' (1979, pp. 39–40).

social comparison processes I have previously mentioned Festinger's theory of social comparison processes which proposes that *individuals* compare themselves with others in order to establish or validate their behaviour or attitudes, particularly where 'objective' criteria are lacking. Tajfel and Turner (1979) argue that an equivalent process takes place in *groups* and that every group needs to maintain a positive social indentity *vis-à-vis* other social groups. They conceive of groups as a collection of individuals who *perceive themselves* to be members of the same social category. They look on social categorizations as resulting from *cognitive processes* which allow individuals to classify and order the environment and which enable them to define their own place in society. Social groups hence provide their members with an identification of themselves in social terms. Thus, social groups may be conceptualized as a number of individuals who share a common social identification of themselves (Turner, 1982) and group behaviour may be conceived as dependent on, and arising from, the functioning of such shared social identifications. Through the process of identifying with a particular group and categorizing oneself as a member, one may be said to develop a social identity (see section 3.4).

In this view, by competing with, and by discriminating against, members of other groups, individuals can create and maintain a positive image of their own group, and hence of themselves. This, as Tajfel and his colleagues have demonstrated, is true even of minimal ephemeral groups who, perhaps precisely because of the lack of an objective reality, have to engage in social comparisons with the other group in order to establish a social identity. Social categorization, identification with a group, the formation of a social identity, enhanced ingroup feeling and discrimination against the outgroup in this view are all part of the same basic cognitive processes. Tajfel and Turner (1979) think that Sherif's work on intergroup behaviour, by focusing on real conflicts between groups, has neglected to explore the processes which lead to ingroup identification in the first place. Sherif, as we have seen, viewed ingroup identification as largely the *consequence* of a real conflict between groups. Tajfel and Turner (1979), by contrast, address themselves to the exploration of the psychological processes which lead to the development of such positive ingroup identification. As we shall see in the next section, their starting point is the distinction between two kinds of social behaviour, *interpersonal* and *intergroup behaviour*, and two kinds of identities, *personal* and *social identity*.

3.4 Personal and social identities

interpersonal behaviour Tajfel and Turner (1979) describe, at one extreme of a continuum, *interpersonal* behaviour which is based on purely personal relationships and the characteristics of the interacting individuals, such as those of a pair of close friends or of husband and wife (though they may well have come together because they belonged to the same 'social categories' – class, neighbourhood, firm or club). But, even in these intensely personal relationships, once they cease to be wholly satisfactory, quarrels or abuse tend to be in terms of social categories – 'Just like a woman' or 'I cannot stand your lower-middle-class attitudes'. Of course, where people use such social categories, it may be because they are afraid to make a quarrel too personal. It is easier and less final, to say 'Just like a woman' than to say 'Just like you'.

intergroup behaviour At the other extreme Tajfel and Turner see *intergroup* behaviour as largely determined by the group memberships of the interacting individuals. Thus, the personal characteristics of a shop steward and a foreman or of members of the CBI and the TUC would *not* be the main determinants of their interactions. Their relationships will be primarily characterized by the positions they will take because of their group memberships and 'mandates' from these groups. The members of the two interacting groups will perceive each other largely in terms of their group memberships, at any rate for the purposes of their professional interaction – even though a senior union leader and a senior management representative may both live in the same 'bourgeois' lifestyle and have personal characteristics in common. Much work on 'communications' has demonstrated that what people say or write in their capacity as spokespersons for their group members or as expert witnesses is usually pre-judged or misinterpreted by their audiences because the recipients of the communication are aware of its source and guard themselves against unwelcome influences or, as the case may be, are the more willing to listen to the message.

Perceiving people in terms of their group memberships tends to imply a focus on relatively few characteristics which are salient from the point of view of the observer's group. This process of 'stereotyping' simplifies and orders our impressions and perceptions. Without thought or examination we will 'know' the characteristics of people such as 'union leaders' or 'employers' or those of members of a religious or racial or political group since we already have a picture
social identity of them based on our attitudes or prejudices. We attribute to them a 'social identity'. As Berger and Luckman (1967) have argued, social reality is not out there to be simply seen and assimilated but is a *construction* based on preconceptions as well as reflecting the actual events or people which are observed and interpreted. However, stereotyping is not only a cognitive process of simplifying

and structuring our social world, it tends to have the function of differentiating ourselves from outgroups and of justifying actions against such groups.

Turner (1982) makes the further point that individuals stereotype *themselves*, a process he refers to as 'depersonalization'. This allows the individual to 'switch on' or emphasize the different social identities she or he has developed as a member of her or his sex, class and occupation or in the role of wife or husband, 'friend of the earth', feminist or whatever, when these become salient. Such social **personal identity** identity or identities are distinguished by Turner from personal identity, the latter referring to the personal characteristics and attributes which make the individual unique. Inevitably, social identities are not wholly divorced from one's personal identity; one's experience of a social identity (say that of being a member of a profession or a sect) will affect what one is like 'deep down' – one's personal identity. The concepts of personal identity and social identity merely highlight that we may behave (and feel) differently in different situations. The concept of *role*, as we have already seen in the study of prisoners and guards, has the same explanatory aim and power.

Turner sees the switch in self-concept from personal to social identity as corresponding to and responsible for a shift from interpersonal to intergroup behaviour with its concomitant stereotypic perception both of the members of the ingroup and of those in the outgroup. Do you think of yourself as a Scot as contrasted with an English person? Or as a woman as contrasted with a man? Or as a member of the engineering department as contrasted with members of the sales department? When you think of yourself in such ways do you attribute to yourself certain (limited) characteristics which you think are typical of the Scots, of women, of engineers? If you do, then you are thinking of yourself in terms of your social identities (or, to refer back to concepts we used earlier, to the perceived identities of your reference groups) rather than in terms of your idiosyncratic features as an individual. At times, when such social identities are salient, your interactions will be in terms of your group membership both within your group and towards the outgroup. The crucial statement here is, of course, 'when they are salient'. A fight or an argument between several people may be purely interpersonal. On the other hand, it may have started as or become an intergroup affair because the opponents see themselves as members of two groups – black and white, or picket line and strike breakers – though in other situations the *same* people may interact peacefully or, for that matter, have an interpersonal argument. Thus, even where groups are involved in a conflict, not all occasions when members of such groups meet up with each other are categorized as intergroup situations. However, the longer the history of a conflict or the more intense it is, the more likely is it that any interactions are viewed as 'intergroup' rather than 'interpersonal' encounters. In other words, the long-standing intergroup conflict becomes so salient that it affects all relationships and encounters.

Is the distinction between personal and social identities useful beyond the descriptive level? Group membership and, therefore, social identities become salient at times of threat or conflict, as the Sherifs (1953) and many others have demonstrated, or when norms are challenged by new experiences (as Minard's study (1952) of the coal-miners' attitudes below and above ground has indicated in Box 14) or when people are faced by uncertainty or ambiguity (as Asch (1955) has shown). We would, therefore, expect intergroup behaviour to be more hostile or competitive than interpersonal behaviour (and Turner's formulation might alert us to this) and the hostility to be less capable of reduction since hostility towards the outgroup is accompanied by an increased sense of belongingness to the ingroup and the over-evaluation of its members.

Brown and Turner (1981) are also concerned to demonstrate that it is inherently difficult to extrapolate from theories of interpersonal behaviour to the explanation of intergroup behaviour. They criticize two influential positions which have attempted to do so, Rokeach's 'belief congruence theory' and so-called 'contact theorists'.

belief congruence theory   They first examine Rokeach's belief congruence theory (Rokeach, 1960, 1968) which proposes that the similarity or congruence between the belief systems of individuals is an important determinant of their attitudes towards each other and that similarities and differences between people's beliefs are more important for their mutual acceptance or rejection than their group membership. Specifically, whilst this theory could be applied to discrimination against any outgroup, Rokeach focused on discrimination against racially or ethnically distinct outgroups. Rokeach explains race prejudice as an outcome of perceived or assumed belief incongruence. His research (and that of others, for instance, Byrne (1971) whose work was referred to in Unit 10/11) seems to establish that individual white subjects (students from one university in the north and from one in the south of the United States) are usually more attracted to black subjects to whom *similar* beliefs are attributed than to white subjects to whom different beliefs are attributed by the researcher. Brown and Turner point out that belief congruence is a theory of interpersonal attraction; it is therefore without implications for explaining prejudice and racism which represent intergroup behaviour and which tend to follow established social norms for intergroup behaviour. Furthermore, one might add, the findings were obtained in the laboratory (as, indeed, were Turner's), away from social contexts and social pressures. Racism and prejudice, however, are *social* problems and not a temporary response in a laboratory by an *individual*. In Rokeach's paradigm people were likely to be perceived as unique individuals and not as members of outgroups. In consequence, a person may be preferred to another (because she or he holds similar beliefs) without this generalizing to their (racial) outgroup as a whole. Indeed, what subjects in this situation do is to create for themselves a satisfactory social, as well as personal, identity by making the person with similar beliefs a member of their own (reference) group. However, as soon as other aspects become salient to individuals, for instance in a situation of racial conflict, other attitudes and stereotypical views come to predominate. Thus, it will probably be difficult to start up an inter-racial club in a situation where there has been tension and conflict between racial groups as this will have had the effect of accentuating ingroup evaluation and outgroup rejection (even though the assumption would be that the club serves the needs and interests of several racial groups). In a different sort of emotional climate, however, interpersonal relations, possibly based on belief similarities or common interest, can cut across racial or other divisions precisely because the new group (for instance, a club for keen amateur photographers) becomes more salient than other factors (such as racial divisions) and new norms governing the interpersonal relations in the club will evolve. In such a situation, of course, we may expect belief similarity to develop as a new group norm or, equally likely, members will *assume* that such similarity exists and hence are likely to perceive it.

contact theory   Secondly, Brown and Turner (1981) also question the underlying assumptions of contact theorists that contact between members of different groups, on an equal status basis and backed by wider social norms or legislation, will lead to a reduction in prejudice and discrimination. This view was advocated by Allport (1954) in his seminal book on prejudice, and is reflected by, amongst others, Pettigrew (1971), Minard (1952) and Deutsch and Collins (1951).

We have already seen in discussing the experiments of the Sherifs (1953) and their colleagues that *mere contact* heightened rather than reduced intergroup conflict. Deutsch and Collins (1951), however, found that in racially integrated housing estates (a new social initiative when they carried out their research) more and friendlier contacts were made between the members of the different racial groups than in segregated estates (even though all the families lived there only because they had no choice and endeavoured to move as soon as they could). However, the matter is not so simple. Was there a *general* reduction in prejudice by white people or did the improved attitudes relate only to specific black neighbours? Would these new attitudes persist (become 'internalized' in Kelman's phrase) if people moved away? If they did persist, would the effect be due to contact or to a more general change in the norms of the wider society as a result of new laws or education or improved employment prospects? We have already noted that Minard (1952) found reductions in prejudice at the workplace where they were sanctioned by unions and employers, but not to the same extent in the wider community where segregation was still usual. Amir (1969) points out that interracial attitudes were improved markedly when blacks and whites served side by side in battle or on ships during World War II (though their relationships at base camp were not so good). Thus, personal contact and superordinate goals, as well as sharing dangers, seem to have contributed to improved relationships.

Brown and Turner (1981) in discussing contact theorists make the point that intergroup contact *can* reduce conflict or prejudice but not because it encourages *interpersonal* friendships (as Deutsch and Collins might argue) but because contact changes the nature and structure of the intergroup relationship. Hence, in fact, whilst analytically distinct, there may be a continuum between interpersonal and intergroup behaviour, just as there is also a continuum between personal and social identities.

In conclusion, we need to note that in real life it may not usually be possible to establish whether discriminatory intergroup behaviour is based on 'real' conflict or on attempts to achieve distinctiveness for one's own group. This is so because, outside the laboratory, distinctiveness for one's own group tends to be achieved by setting oneself apart from those others who are already in some sense different from oneself or one's group. Whether these differences are between the skilled and the unskilled, the Scots and the English, or black and white people, once these categorizations and distinctions have been made they tend to become 'institutionalized' and part of the culture and ideology of these groups. Where there are tangible economic reasons for continuing them they tend to be even more difficult to dislodge and the economic differences may, of course, be the result of long-term discrimination.

If competition with, and discrimination against, the outgroup encourages positive ingroup feelings (and this is something people apparently value), can ingroup feelings be achieved in socially acceptable ways, for instance by peaceful competition in sport, particularly in team sports, through competition between work teams or between school 'houses'? The difficulty here is two-fold. One, the psychological satisfaction of ingroup belongingness seems almost inevitably also to lead to stereotypic and hostile perceptions of the outgroup and it is difficult to strike a healthy balance. Two, and equally or even more importantly, there may come a point where the participants in opposing groups or teams can see that they are being exploited. Thus in industry, *group incentives*, where people are interdependent on each other or where there is competition between several teams, tend to work better than *individual incentives* (in terms of output *and* job satisfaction) but only so long as both management and workers share the same perceptions and agree that increased productivity (their joint superordinate goal) is what they all aspire to. Once they do not, for instance when workers believe that increased output will lead to rate-cutting or unemployment, incentives, whether based on individual or group effort, tend to cease to have any effect at all.

Superordinate goals may be effective in eliminating conflicts between groups *within* a society; it would also appear that diverse groups can be rallied to the same cause if a target group *outside* the immediate situation or the society can be identified. Such is the paradox of human nature and society that the obscenity of war can be a psychologically uplifting experience: a socially acceptable outgroup is identified and ingroup feeling is enhanced.[5] In Freudian terms, as you will know from your Set Book on Freud (Stevens, 1983, chapter 5) and from our discussion of ego-defensive attitudes, aggression can be directed towards and displaced onto a socially sanctioned target without arousing the guilt feelings which so often accompany aggression against other targets such as members of one's own family.

3.5 Is intergroup conflict inevitable?

The work of Tajfel and his colleagues seems to demonstrate quite conclusively that people value group membership *per se* and that to experience a positive social identity their own group must be capable of differentiation from other groups. This, in turn, leads to discrimination against members of the outgroup because the discriminatory strategies adopted will establish a distinction between the ingroup and the outgroup which in turn enhances a positive social identity.

But are these phenomena universal? The generality of the phenomenon has been examined in England and in Europe with, on the whole, results which confirm the original findings. Wetherall's (1982) study in New Zealand shows the effect of different cultural values: see Box 15.

Box 15   Cross-cultural studies of minimal groups (Wetherall, 1982)

Wetherall, however, showed that the discriminatory behaviour found in the 'minimal' group situation can be influenced by cultural norms, an explanation which had previously been discounted and rejected by Tajfel and his co-workers. Wetherall conducted a series of 'minimal' group experiments with Polynesian and white children in New Zealand schools. She found that both groups displayed ingroup bias in the allocation of rewards but that the Polynesian children moderated their discrimination, displaying greater generosity to the outgroup.

She explains these findings by pointing out that Polynesians in New Zealand had maintained their native cultural institutions which are based on cooperation, particularly among members of the extended family. A person's status among Polynesians is associated with the extent of her or his generosity. For Polynesians to distinguish themselves and their group from others may, therefore, in such experiments as well as in real life, depend on being generous to them (rather than discriminating against them as the European groups did). Thus, the cultural values and norms of these children (contrary to Tajfel's original expectations) influenced their behaviour towards the outgroup in the experimental situation.

We might speculate, therefore, that discrimination towards outgroups is not inevitable, *provided* we can learn to be more cooperative and to change our social institutions and structures to encourage cooperation rather than competition. This point is further discussed in section 3.7.

3.6   Bystander apathy

In section 3.3 we saw how easy it is to establish ingroups and outgroups in the laboratory and how these divisions need not stem from historical events, present attitudes or 'real' conflicts between groups. The mere division of people into groups on a quite arbitrary basis can lead to discrimination against those not perceived as of one's own group, though Wetherall's research (section 3.5) showed that cultural norms may temper this tendency. But the question 'Who do you include in your group?' is one we need to explore further. I have raised this very same question when discussing Milgram's experiments (section 1.4). It is all very well to 'explain' the findings by stating that the subjects obeyed authority. But, *why* did they do this and *why* was the 'victim' considered an outsider to whom no compassion was owed? Perhaps we can gain some insight into these questions by considering the following real event and the research it generated.

bystander apathy

Kitty Genovese was murdered in 1964 in Queens, one of the five boroughs which make up New York City. She was on her way home from a night job in the early hours of the morning when she was stabbed repeatedly over an extended period of time. Thirty-eight residents of this respectable New York City neighbourhood admitted to having witnessed at least part of the attack but none went to her aid or called the police until after she was dead. This 'bystander apathy', as it came to be called, caught the imagination and concern of social psychologists and provided the impetus for more than a decade of research which explored the conditions in which a bystander comes to offer assistance to or withholds it from an unknown person who needs help unexpectedly. In other words, in what sort of circumstances and through what sort of psychological processes will a bystander come to include a stranger into her or his ingroup and offer help? Initially, the focus of research was on the determinants of *non*-intervention, starting with the research by Latané and Darley (1970) which is reported in their book *The Unresponsive Bystander: Why Does He Not Help?* Later the emphasis switched to understanding altruism and helping behaviour in crises or emergencies.

altruism

Altruism should be defined in terms of acts that objectively provide no benefit to and often cause harm or distress to the actor while benefiting another. However, strictly speaking, such selfless acts may nevertheless be rewarding to the actor in the sense that she or he may be living up to her or his self-image as a caring person. There is also the possibility that apparently altruistic acts are a form of defence against aggressive impulses which need to be kept in check to aid a person's self-esteem.

In the context of research on bystander apathy, helping behaviour in crises or emergencies tends to be seen as the intervention by the amateur or bystander rather than the help or assistance given by the professional – doctor, nurse, police or firefighter – who are formally and professionally required to give help.

Psychologists have asked many questions about bystander intervention or apathy. What processes are at work which lead to an individual's decision to go to the aid (or not) of someone else in an emergency? How do individuals *perceive* such situations, how do they *feel* in the situation, how do they judge the *victim*, how do they assess the *costs* of intervention? However, here we can only focus on two aspects of this more general phenomenon: one, how is ingroup feeling generated between the victim and the bystander?; and, two, how is this process affected by the presence of other bystanders – does such a presence lead to ingroup feelings between the bystanders rather than between the bystander and the victim? See Box 16.

ACTIVITY 9

Have you ever been in such a situation? How did you react? Can you recall your feelings at the time? Do the explanations given below by Latané and Darley make sense to you in the light of your own experience?

---

diffusion of responsibility

Latané and Darley (1970, 1976) suggested that the presence of other bystanders can affect an individual's response to an emergency in three ways. First of all, the presence of others may allow the *responsibility* for helping to be diffused among the group (since there are others who could help). Equally the guilt and blame for not helping may be diffused (and thus the psychological costs to the individual of not helping reduced).[6] Secondly, the reaction of other bystanders to an emergency provides *information* to the individual: the passive stooge gives the subject the impression that the situation is less severe than she or he might think. Thirdly, concern for the evaluation which others might make of her or him (*normative* social influence) can affect a bystander's likelihood of intervention.

Both the second and third point involve social comparison processes. The 'diffusion hypothesis' generated a considerable volume of research. Piliavin *et al.* (1981) who reviewed these studies point out that there is some confusion about

Box 16   Research on bystander apathy (Latané and Darley, 1968; Latané and Rodin, 1969)

In their first study, Latané and Darley used an experimental situation which involved the subjects hearing someone apparently having a severe epileptic-like fit in another room. In the experimental room, subjects (who had been enlisted to take part in an ostensibly quite different research project) found themselves either alone or with four other subjects. The results were quite unequivocal: those subjects who were alone when the victim (apparently) had a seizure in the next room were much more likely to go to his aid and, on average, reacted in less than one-third of the time as compared to those subjects who were in the company of others.

Epileptic fits are perhaps not very common events and so Latané and Rodin (1969) set up a further study in which subjects heard someone (apparently) fall of a ladder in the next room and moan. The experiment was carried out under four conditions: subjects were:
1   alone;
2   two friends together;
3   two strangers together; or,
4   the subject was with an experimenter's confederate instructed not to intervene.
Seventy per cent of subjects who were alone responded to the situation within sixty-five seconds. Two friends together did nearly as well. When two strangers were together fewer of them reacted and their reaction was much slower. Those subjects who were in the presence of the passive collaborator of the experimenter showed the least and the slowest reaction.

this concept. They argue that diffusion of responsibility occurs when responsibility is accepted by the subject but *shared* by all the onlookers. They distinguish 'diffusion of responsibility' from 'dissolution of responsibility' which, they say, occurs when the behaviour of other bystanders cannot be observed and the subject 'rationalizes' that someone else has already helped. Whatever label is attached to the process almost all the studies reveal the inhibitory effect of the presence of others. There is a limit to such diffusion though: Piliavin and his colleagues found that help was forthcoming on crowded subway trains as frequently as on relatively empty ones. Perhaps it is more difficult to refuse help in a face-to-face situation as LaPiere (Block 5) also found. It is also possible that in an enclosed space like a subway carriage a feeling of 'common fate' among the passengers and hence of ingroup membership is generated. The notion, originally proposed by Latané and Darley (1970), that informational social influence, normative social influence and diffusion of responsibility are dynamically distinct processes is upheld by several independent investigations (for instance, by Schwartz and Gottlieb, 1976). Informational social influence (a cognitive process) primarily affects the bystander's *interpretation* of a situation; diffusion of responsibility occurs later, as does normative social influence which relates to concern about the evaluation by others of one's action, that is, whether one *should* or *should not* intervene.

dissolution of responsibility

informational social influence
normative social influence

Bystanders, then, have an effect on each other – but do the characteristics of the *victim* also influence the readiness of a bystander to intervene? As we have already seen in earlier sections it is very easy to engender ingroup favouritism and a feeling of 'we-ness'. Not surprisingly, therefore, many studies found that similarity between victim and bystander and physical closeness to the victim increases the potential for arousal of the bystander's sympathy and the extent to which assistance is forthcoming. The psychological costs for helping a victim should also be less for similar than dissimilar victims as the bystander would be more confident of the consequences associated with interacting with a similar victim. One implication of this tends to be that the greater the distress or injury, deformity or unusualness of the victim the less are we likely to perceive her or him as like us and the less help is extended. There is evidence for this point from experiments. For instance, a victim of a (staged) subway emergency who has an unattractive birthmark is less likely to receive help than one who does not have such a mark (Piliavin, Piliavin and Rodin, 1975) and the victim receives more help if he is not bleeding from the mouth than if he is (Piliavin and Piliavin, 1972), presumably because the sight of such 'stigmatized' victims is too horrifying and offputting, and sympathy is inhibited by defence mechanisms. Other studies showed that a stranded motorist who is dressed and groomed neatly is far more likely to receive help than one whose clothing is casual and whose hair is long (Graf and Riddell, 1972).

Since most of the bystander research has been carried out in the United States there are quite a few studies which focus on the effect of race on bystander intervention. Are racially similar victims helped more readily than dissimilar ones? The evidence is inconclusive and Piliavin et al. (1981) suggest that, irrespective of their racial attitudes, people may be concerned with projecting a nonbigoted self-image, do not consider themselves as prejudiced (even if they score highly on prejudice on attitude scales) and hence would not easily act negatively towards someone merely on the basis of a person's race. In other words, if white people do not help black people, or vice versa, additional psychological costs (such as loss of self-esteem) may be incurred. Other characteristics of the victim may cross-cut with race. Thus, Piliavin, Rodin and Piliavin (1969) varied two victim characteristics: race (black versus white) and source of the problem (illness versus drunkenness) when the victim collapsed in a subway train. Only with the drunk victim was a race effect obtained, not with the apparently disabled victim using a cane. They suggest that the costs for not helping were lower for the drunk (since he was perceived as less like oneself, less deserving and his condition as less likely to be serious and indeed self-inflicted) and, in that condition, his race was also weighed in the balance by the potential helper. However, these *post hoc* explanations for the experimental findings may not be universally true.

Whilst our quick glance at victim-helper interactions has limited itself to exploring the reactions of the casual bystander I cannot resist the temptation to draw your attention to some studies which show that professional helpers, too, distinguish between victims on a variety of criteria and that the help they extend is influenced by how they categorize the victim. For instance, Sudnow (1973) in California and also Simpson (1976) in London show that if the ambulance crew or the staff in the emergency room think someone is dead or as good as dead, then fewer resuscitation attempts are initiated than if he is categorized as needing help urgently. Which category the patient is put in may depend on age. Thus, lack of vital signs of life will be taken at face value if the patient is elderly: the patient will be assumed to be 'dead on arrival' and no attempts to resuscitate her or him will be made. However, the same symptoms in a younger person may be viewed as cardiac arrest, so resuscitation attempts are commenced immediately by the ambulance crew who will race to the hospital and alert the emergency room whilst still on the way.

Simpson (1976) also showed that a patient's presumed moral character may determine the category into which she or he is put. Thus, someone smelling of alcohol (particularly if also shabbily dressed or unwashed), drug addicts, prostitutes, vagrants, persons injured in fights and attempted suicides are less often judged to need urgent attention. Simpson argues that hospital personnel seem to feel that such persons are less deserving of help (just like the drunk person in the subway experiment) than those of a 'higher moral character'. He advises that the best way to survive a heart attack is to 'Look as young as you can, dress well and traditionally, disguise your deviances and keep your breath fresh' (Simpson, 1976, p. 248).

I have in this section from time to time referred to the psychological costs incurred by the helper. But is help always welcome to the victims? Do they incur costs in accepting help? There is, of course, no evidence for answering this question from the studies mentioned here since the situations in which the bystanders' behaviour was observed were all ingeniously faked (in the laboratory or in ecologically more valid settings such as in a subway train or in a street) and there were no genuine victims. However, we know, for instance from the hostile way in which foreign aid is often received, that there are psychological costs incurred by the recipients which need to be hidden from consciousness by directing hostility rather than thanks towards the provider. In interpersonal relationships, too, we can be embarrassed by too much generosity. Exchange theory (discussed in Unit 10/11, section 3) would predict that we try to maintain a balance of favours, gifts or help given and received so that we feel at ease. This may, in part, explain why people are so reluctant to accept welfare or social work intervention which they view, negatively, as charity.

3.7   Conclusions to section 3

I do not want to rehearse here, once more, the arguments and conclusions outlined in this section. But, as in my comments at the end of section 1 about the nature of ingroup phenomena and processes, I must stress that the various explanations advanced here for understanding intergroup relations and conflicts are not mutually exclusive. Each approach – whether based on the importance of incompatible goals, on hostile attitudes and prejudice, on stereotyping and scapegoating, on 'minimal' groups or on the distinction between and consequences of personal and social identities – seems to chip away at part only of the unknown. The important unknown (not just for social psychology but for mankind) is how we can achieve more inclusive groups or better intergroup relations. On the one hand, we might think of changes in socialization and education. Some support for such a view is given by the study of Wetherall (1982) which was discussed in section 3.5. Her work showed that the norms children acquire in their society guide their reactions to the outgroup. On the other h .nd, we need to place these findings against the evidence from other studies mentioned in this Block, which seem to indicate not only the importance to people of membership in *small* groups but the enhancement of the psychological pleasure of membership through setting one's own group off against another. As I pointed out towards the end of section 3.4, people seem to manage to feel at one with large groupings, such as a nation, mainly when there is an external enemy, which is not a very reassuring conclusion to arrive at if one is interested in peaceful coexistence.

But even if the psychological evidence all pointed in the same direction most social problems (such as racial prejudice or other intergroup conflicts) cannot be solved at the psychological level alone. We have seen, for instance, that racial prejudice stems mainly from the norms of a society rather than from the psychological quirks of individuals (section 3.2). Such norms tend to reflect the long-term economic or legal disadvantages which may have created or contributed to the very differences which continue to feed the prejudiced norms. To change such norms, then, one cannot simply operate on the psychological level and change the content of education or socialization with a view to creating less prejudiced attitudes. Important as this is, one may also need to change the economic and political position of disadvantaged groups. Thus the legal system of a country will need to provide for and enforce non-discrimination in housing, in job opportunities, in access to education and so on. The legal framework embodies and defines what a society considers proper and moral and, in turn, will have effects on behaviour (by discouraging discrimination) as well as on attitudes, at least over a period of time. Perhaps we can put this argument another way. Throughout this Block we have seen that it is not necessarily the individual who is aggressive to others or unresponsive to their needs but that she or he is in situations which allow, or indeed propel, them to behave in such a way. This perhaps is the real message of Milgram. To effect change, then, we need to focus on the social institutions of a society as well as on its people.

It is precisely because change needs to proceed on both these fronts, the personal and the social, that intervention is so difficult and is likely to have unintended consequences. Throughout your Course Reader (Murphy, John and Brown, 1984), though especially in chapter 2, we point to these problems. We also point there, as I have done in this Block, to the doubtful validity or time-bound nature of much social psychological research. This should make us cautious in applying findings in new contexts unless we carefully monitor the outcomes.

4 CROWDS

In the English language (and presumably in other languages, too) there are words which have an unpleasant or derogatory connotation. Thus 'trade union boss' as compared to 'trade union leader' has nasty overtones and the same can be said of 'capitalist' as compared to 'entrepreneur' or 'employer'. The use of the word 'regime' rather than 'government' is always intended to suggest repression or illegality and 'propaganda' tends not to be equated with 'education'. 'Crowds' in contrast to 'groups' is also one of these emotive terms. It suggests danger, uncontrollable violence, riots, vandalism, lynchings or other apparently irrational behaviours. It has this connotation in part, no doubt, because crowds *can* be destructive and violent but, in part, because a book by Le Bon, published originally in 1895 and still in print, set the scene with a most unflattering analysis of crowd phenomena. Le Bon stressed three characteristics of the crowd:

anonymity (a) *anonymity* which he sees as leading to irresponsibility;

contagion (b) *contagion* to others in the crowd which he sees as leading to a sacrifice of self-interest and of personal standards and to the creation of 'homogeneity' among the members of a crowd;

suggestibility (c) *suggestibility* which to him implied that the conscious personality has vanished and the 'racial unconscious' had taken over.

Many of these alleged attributes of the crowd still inform current research though Le Bon's explanations of the processes operating in the crowd are not necessarily accepted. In particular, no one would nowadays think of suggestibility in terms of the *racial* unconscious (though Freud (1921) suggests that the crowd allows expression of normally *repressed* behaviour).

Le Bon wrote against the background of the events of the French Revolution but also in the aftermath of the French defeat in the 1870 Franco-Prussian war, the 'insurrection' of the Paris Commune and the rise of socialism in France. His ideas parallel those developed by sociologists of that period and later who basically saw 'mass society' as the result of the breakdown of normal constraints and the crowd as a pathological aggregate of people – a mob – in which individuals lose their identity.

Le Bon's ideas have fascinated many social psychologists including Freud (who refers to Le Bon in his *Group Psychology and the Analysis of the Ego*, 1921) from very early days to the present. (For an excellent review of the history of these ideas see Reicher (1982).) Crowds, of course, have again become a topical subject in the wake of mass protests and urban riots in many countries since the 1960s and the increase in vandalism and football hooliganism. Several questions therefore pose themselves. Have contemporary social psychologists been successful in providing a framework within which such collective actions can be analysed and understood? Do we understand the social contexts in which they occur? Are crowds always hostile or aggressive? Do we have some understanding of what it feels like to be in a crowd, be that a rioting mob or the crowd celebrating New Year's Eve in Trafalgar Square? Can we relate the analysis of crowds to that of groups or to other areas of social psychology? For instance, will we again find evidence of pressures towards conformity or the diffusion of responsibility? Will the concept of 'social identity' help us to understand crowd behaviours? Do we understand how crowds come together and are mobilized? Do crowds have leaders?

Most writers in using the term crowd refer to a spontaneous, sudden aggregation of people rather than an assembly of people in a predetermined place such as a congregation in church or people attending an advertised political meeting. *The Times* of 2 June 1982, reports: 'The Pope faced a *congregation* of 300 000 . . .' (emphasis added). The *number* of people is, therefore, not necessarily a factor in defining crowds, though the anonymity of the individual amongst a large number of people has often been used as an explanation of crowd behaviour. One of the aspects which has been studied, mainly by sociologists, concerns the speed with which a crowd can be mobilized, for instance in response to alleged police provocation. The cues and messages and the channels of communication through which potential participants may be alerted are, therefore, also relevant to a description and analysis of a crowd.

However, not all writers limit themselves to spontaneous, initially structureless assemblies when analysing crowds. Because of the association of the word crowd with collective violence, many researchers focus on gangs or similar groupings which have an existence over an extended period of time. Thus the football 'crowd' may consist of rival gangs or rival supporters' groups with their own structures and rituals in which 'aggro' or violence may have a predetermined role. Collective violence may also be a well thought-out strategy in political protest and apparently spontaneous crowds may, in fact, have been carefully brought together, briefed and led. As we shall see, social psychologists tend to focus on understanding the psychological changes or processes occurring in people in crowds, whilst sociologists tend to focus on the social contexts in which crowds take action, spontaneously or otherwise. In the next sections we shall look at some of the studies which have been undertaken to gain an understanding of crowd behaviour and we shall relate these findings to our study of groups.

4.1 Deindividuation

For Le Bon the important question was why individuals in a crowd behave in ways which are uncharacteristic of them as individuals. Fromm (1941) thought of individuality and a sense of self-awareness and uniqueness as human attributes which have emerged over a long historical period, a development which, whilst it makes people 'free', may also isolate them from each other and make them fear their freedom. Fromm, therefore, sought to understand what motivates some people to submerge their individuality in groups.

deindividuation The concept of deindividuation relates to both these questions. It was Festinger, Pepitone and Newcomb (1952) who, deriving the idea from Le Bon, first postulated the concept of deindividuation which they define 'as a state of affairs in a group where members do not pay attention to other individuals *qua* individuals and, correspondingly, the members do not feel they are being singled out by others' (p. 389). Such a state may lead to a reduction of inner constraints for group members and facilitate behaviour which would normally be inhibited. The authors carried out research on laboratory groups, not real crowds, though they expected their findings to throw light on behaviour in crowds. They postulated that groups provide two kinds of satisfaction for their members: at times, satisfaction may derive from one or more individuals being singled out in the group and accorded prestige or status, and hence group membership facilitates ego identity: at other times, satisfaction may be derived from the precise opposite, that is deindividuation or the merging of the individual into the group. Box 16 outlines Festinger *et al*'s (1952) experiment to explore deindividuation.

Box 16   Deindividuation in a group (Festinger *et al.*, 1952)

Festinger *et al.* set out to demonstrate the existence of deindividuation by creating a situation in which group members might be tempted to express anti-parent statements (perhaps not quite as common an occurrence in the late 1940s as it may be today). Briefly, the experimenters ran a number of discussion groups for male undergraduate volunteers. They were asked to discuss their own feelings towards their parents after reading a fictitious survey indicating that eighty-seven per cent of a representative student population possessed a strong deep-seated hatred of one or both parents and that those who denied at first that they had such feelings or were reluctant to discuss them were subsequently diagnosed as possessing the most violent forms of hostility. (This latter statement was included to put pressure on members to admit to such feelings and to discuss them.)

Festinger and his colleagues found a correlation between the frequency with which negative statements about parents were made and the extent to which their subjects failed to remember who said what in a post-discussion test. They concluded that these results indicated support for their contention that deindividuation leads to a reduction of inhibitions. They found, also, that those groups in which there had been more expression of hostility towards parents were more attractive to their members (as expressed in the willingness to return for further discussions on this topic) and hence that 'submergence' in the group can be thought of as one of the satisfactions to be gained from group membership.

However, one might well argue that deindividuation may *follow* from uninhibited behaviour in groups, rather than be the cause of it. The similarity between group members may increase and less attention be paid to individuals as they engage in unrestrained behaviour. Perhaps because Festinger *et al.*'s study was somewhat unconvincing it took more than a decade before a second was done. Singer, Brush and Lublin (1965) placed stress on internal psychological processes rather than on group membership by defining deindividuation as a 'subjective state in which people lose their self-consciousness' (p. 356). They found in their study that deindividuation led to a larger number of obscene comments being made by their female subjects in conditions of anonymity when discussing pornography, and that this increased deindividuation was again complemented by a greater liking for the group.

Zimbardo (1969), in a very influential paper, also focused on the absence of self-awareness and self-evaluation coupled with lowered concern for social evaluation in the state of deindividuation. He saw deindividuation as a complex process in which (a) certain situational conditions lead to (b) an internal deindividuated state in which the individual changes her or his perception of her- or himself and of others and (c) engages in relatively uninhibited behaviour whether this is antisocial *or* 'positive' (such as the expression of intense feelings of happiness or sorrow).

Zimbardo, again following Le Bon, proposed *anonymity* as a major source of deindividuation. He was the first to operationalize anonymity by masking and hooding his subjects, a technique frequently copied later by other researchers. Zimbardo, however, found it difficult to manipulate anonymity. For instance, in an experiment with troops drawn from the Belgian Army, non-identifiability, or loss of personal identity, was again assumed to be created by the soldiers wearing hoods covering their heads. However, the expected results of increased aggression by the deindividuated soldiers was not obtained because the soldiers, unaccustomed as they were to being hooded, became self-conscious, suspicious and anxious. They may have *looked* deindividuated to the experimenter but the results indicated they were not. By contrast, the apparently non-deindividuated subjects in the control group retained the 'normal' extent of deindividuation resulting from their status as uniformed soldiers. Indeed, uniforms tend to be imposed – in the army, schools, convents, monasteries, prisons or on hospital patients or hospital staff – to reduce individuality. As Goffman (1968, 1971) has so graphically described, we need our personal possessions, including our clothes and room furnishings to present ourselves to the world and to maintain our identity as individuals. Uniforms, then, may increase deindividuation (but they may also assist team effort by presenting a symbol of the common endeavour which binds the group together).

Zimbardo's studies were followed by a considerable number of others but, as Diener (1980) points out, the experimental evidence remains inconclusive and the manipulation of anonymity at times interacts with other variables in unpredictable ways. This should not surprise us if we accept Zimbardo's view, outlined above, that deindividuation involves prior conditions, a state of mind and the resulting behaviour. Deindividuation is a matter of degree, whichever aspect of this tripartite concept we focus on.

It would appear, then, that the notion of deindividuation, whether or not it arises from anonymity, does not help us very much with understanding behaviour in crowds. Since we are discussing *crowds* in the context of a Block on *groups* we may well ask whether the concept of deindividuation applies to the analysis of processes in groups? In discussing the effects of group membership, I have not used this concept (nor does anyone else seem to use it in this context). We might think that any degree of even routine conformity to group norms could be categorized (or castigated) as being due to a lack of self-awareness, or as involving the loss of some individuality or self-regulation. These terms, as I have pointed out, have all been used to describe deindividuation. The reason why deindividuation has not entered the vocabulary of the study of groups is probably due to the compartmentalization of social psychological research but possibly also due to the fact that the notion of deindividuation came on to the scene when a vocabulary of group phenomena was already well established.

There is also, of course, a somewhat different emphasis when social psychologists study groups and when they study deindividuation. In the former case, they seek to explore how an individual can adapt to a group, maintain her or his individuality and escape from conformity pressures. In the latter case, psychologists accepted, perhaps more readily, that group membership could imply a loss of individuality and sought to explore the precise conditions in which it occurred. However, as we have seen, the first researchers who used the term deindividuation (Festinger *et al.*, 1952) were aware of these complex interactions between the individual and her or his group and emphasized that identification with the group may strengthen ego identification in certain circumstances, and in others it may reduce it and the self become deindividuated and 'submerged' in the group.

There is also the question of how and why people get themselves into situations of deindividuation (apart from laboratory experiments to which they are lured by some cover story). Certainly, sometimes membership of groups may be sought out actively by individuals who seek to lose their inhibitions by joining therapy groups of one kind or another (although this may be partnered by the desire to emerge with a new personality or individuality). Others may immerse themselves in drug-taking sessions or a riot or participate in short-term transgression of cultural norms by 'letting go' at an office party, a carnival or in tribal ceremonies leading to a state of trance. Other people may seek longer-term solutions to their problems of identity and individuality and become monks or soldiers or join a mass movement (though, of course, other motives also play a part in making such choices).

There is another aspect to deindividuation. Victims of aggression are often 'dehumanized' by starving them, shaving their heads and dressing them in ridiculous and ill-fitting clothes so that they appear less human, and therefore can be transgressed against more easily. Anyone who has ever seen photographs of Nazi concentration camp inmates will appreciate this point. Even the Allied troops who liberated the camps found it difficult to relate to the skeleton-like inmates they found there. Another method of deindividuation or dehumanizing target groups or victims is by developing hostile stereotypes about them which then prevent one from relating to such people as individuals, be they enemies in a war or members of a minority group in one's own country.

An aside can be added here to our earlier discussion of 'minimal groups' (section 3.4). You will recall that in these experiments subjects discriminated in favour of anonymous ingroup members and against equally anonymous outgroup members. Anonymity was deliberately imposed so that individual differences would not influence the reactions of the subjects. From our present context we can see that such depersonalization by imposing anonymity is only a step away from dehumanizing the 'enemy' so that she or he can be better discriminated against.

Anonymity, as we have seen, does not necessarily lead to deindividuation nor can we simply use these concepts in an analysis of crowd phenomena. As Reicher (1984) points out in the article we have included in your Course Reader (Murphy, John and Brown, 1984) on the troubles in the St. Paul's area of Bristol in 1980, members of crowds often know each other and are not anonymous to their immediate neighbours in the crowd. However, crowds may resent the anonymity of their opponents. Under the title 'Fireproof uniforms anger blacks', these paragraphs appeared in *The Times* in a report on some disturbance in the Notting Hill area of London:

> . . . But at least one serious issue is likely to be raised as a result of the disturbance, that of the flameproof suits worn by the 100 officers, including some from the Special Patrol Group, who took part in the action. That uniform, combined with a hard helmet and visor, does not include a police serial number, making it difficult for anyone who wishes to identify and complain against an individual officer to pursue a grievance.
>
> A middle-aged West Indian, who refused to give his name, but who was in the Mangrove restaurant when it was raided, said yesterday: 'When they came through the door they looked like zombies, dressed in full black with headgear. All they had was one small stripe saying "police" on it. We could not know in the world who they were, their faces were covered and they had helmets.' . . .
>
> (Hewson, *The Times*, 22 April 1982, p. 2)

Did such anonymity have an effect on the behaviour of the police? We do not know, but the newspaper report suggests that it did have an effect on the perceptions and attitudes of some of the West Indians on the scene and hence may have been a factor in escalating violence.

The concept of deindividuation does not seem particularly appropriate to an explanation of crowd behaviour (even though it gives some explanation of why people may behave in uncharacteristic ways in carefully devised laboratory experiments). Thus, some American studies of riots in Watts in Los Angeles in 1965 clearly show that some people join in to be *noticed*, to become aware of their identity, to feel important (Milgram and Toch, 1969) and hence deindividuation would put the wrong label on their motives and experiences. One might even argue that the concept of deindividuation is unnecessary because there are other established concepts – such as roles – which fit some of the experiments and observations carried out in an effort to understand deindividuation. For instance, another famous study by Zimbardo (Zimbardo *et al.* (1973) discussed in Box 11 in section 2.3.6) in which he and his colleagues set up a simulated prison where subjects were allocated at random to the contrasting roles of 'prisoner' and 'guard' is often referred to in the context of deindividuation research. But, although the authors refer to a loss of personal identity and use the word deindividuation, they do so almost as an afterthought. They describe the prisoners and guards as adopting *roles* and the concept of role which relates actual behaviour to prior expectations of what is appropriate in a given context seems much more useful in accounting for the startlingly different behaviours the 'prisoners' and the 'guards' adopted.

role The concept of role embodies at least three notions:

(a) it refers to norms, expectations, taboos or responsibilities associated with a given *position*, such as that of parent, teacher, manager, physician, ringleader or romantic lover. In this sense, role is something outside the person;

(b) roles can be seen as a person's *conception* of the part she or he is to play in a given position. In that sense, roles are an aspect of the person;

(c) one can look at role *behaviour*, that is, the way people actually behave in given positions (and such behaviour presumably relates to their conception of the role). From this point of view one can describe and, possibly, account for individual differences in meeting socially given norms and expectations.

The concept of role, then, refers to socially given expectations in relation to a particular position in a social structure. As such it is perhaps not suited to the analysis of the crowd which, as we have seen, is often thought of as a spontaneously assembled mass of people who do *not* act in accordance with established norms or in a 'normal' social structure. Nevertheless, the concept of role, by stressing that individuals may behave differently when they assume different roles, is useful and not so different from the concept of social identities which people 'switch on' (section 3.4) according to their perception of the demands of the situation they are in. I shall, therefore, next explore how the notion of social identity has been used in describing and analysing crowds. The question is, is this a concept which can usefully be applied to the explanation of behaviour in crowds as well as in groups?

4.2 Social identity and the crowd

Reicher (1984), in the article I have already mentioned, proposes a model of crowd behaviour which is based on the social identity approach of Tajfel and Turner (Tajfel, 1978; Turner, 1982). He argues that 'a crowd is a form of social group in the sense of a set of individuals who perceive themselves as members of a common social category, or, to put it another way, adopt a common *social* identification'. In an earlier paper he argues that such an identity construction does not take place in a void but in a specific social situation. To quote:

> Consider, once more, a crowd of people watching a fascist rally. To the extent that they identify themselves as anti-fascist, they must then clarify for themselves what it means to be an anti-fascist in that situation. Suppose then that an individual who is seen to fulfil the criteria of being an anti-fascist, perhaps by a badge that he wears or by a slogan that he shouts, picks up a stone and flings it at the rally. That act, or rather the idea that it represents, that of disrupting the fascist rally, can come to be definitional of that particular crowd, resulting in a hail of stones, bricks and slogans upon the members of the fascist gathering.
>
> (Reicher, 1982, pp. 70–1)

Thus, in this view, the crowd's behaviour stems from the adoption by the participants of the common social identity of anti-fascist and their behaviour, in turn, will stem from their knowledge and expectations of how such a social identity can be or should be expressed in a particular situation.

But perhaps one does not have to explain how a social identity is adopted in such a situation. Anti-fascists who come to a meeting of fascists are not there by chance and do, of course, already have a common social identity through their shared objection to fascism. They rarely become anti-fascists on the spot. What needs to be explained is how such attitudes come to be translated into sudden action. One may indeed do so in terms of the concept of social identity by stating that these attitudes become *salient* and that the action of one anti-fascist in flinging a stone has shown how these shared attitudes can be expressed (though those present would not 'normally' throw stones or bricks at anyone).

Other empirical research, however, has shown that the crowd is not necessarily as like-minded as is sometimes supposed. For instance, Stark and her colleagues (Stark *et al.*, 1974) found in analysing 1,850 instances of riot action recorded during the Watts (Los Angeles) riots in 1965 that whereas some people looted, others burned and that these two types of crowd actions took place at different times and in different areas. Should we really consider these different actions, occurring in different locations and at varying times, to be the expression of a common social identity? This is perhaps an unanswerable question.

Nevertheless, Reicher strongly argues for the usefulness of the concept of social identity in explaining the genesis and progress of a recent and relatively small-scale British riot. Certainly, having read his analysis one could not easily fall back on explaining the crowd as a pathological aggregate of people or the behaviour of its members as due to 'primitive' human nature as Le Bon would have it. Scarman, however, in discussing the nature of the 1981 riots in Brixton seems to stress 'primitive human nature' as describing, if not explaining, these events. He states: '... the rioters ... found a ferocious delight in arson, criminal damage to property, and in violent attacks upon the police, the fire brigade, and the ambulance service. Their ferocity, which made no distinction between the police and the rescue services, is perhaps, the most frightening aspect of a terrifying weekend' (Scarman, 1982, p. 77). Unless we have considerable firsthand experience of riots we may not be able to decide whether such riots are due to 'primitive human nature' or the expression of a 'social identity'.

Set reading

S. D. Reicher (1984) 'St. Paul's: a study in the limits of crowd behaviour'.

The author describes, in a specially commissioned article, his research concerning some of the events during the riots in the St. Paul's area of Bristol in 1980. This study is interesting as an account of the views of participants and eyewitnesses and may give you more of the 'flavour' of a riot than the laboratory research I describe. It is also interesting for its attempt to use the notion of *social identity* to explain the spread and geographical limits of the riot. This study is an instance of taking a theoretical concept, derived from laboratory experimentation, and exploring its usefulness as an explanatory tool in the world at large. You can judge for yourselves whether the author wholly succeeds in explaining the phenomena he describes in terms of the concept of social identity.

Such work, we might add, also demonstrates, the interplay between 'pure' and 'applied' research and indicates that theoretical advances may evolve from applied work as well as from pure research.

4.3 The assembly process

So far we have reviewed some social psychological concepts – deindividuation, roles and social identity – to explore how far they help us in understanding what happens once a crowd is assembled. There is, however, another kind of question (which has particularly interested sociologists) about how people get to the scene of action and through what channels they hear about an event or a disturbance. Remember that we are still looking at protesting, rioting or looting crowds rather than at organized, preplanned assemblies, although disturbances and riots can develop out of organized meetings such as an initially 'peaceful' demonstration against war or racism.

We have suggested in the last section that the anti-fascist rioters may be brought together by a common interest and, one may presume, with prior knowledge of the time and place of the fascist meeting. Their presence, therefore, needs no explanation though their actions perhaps do. Much more puzzling are sudden outbursts of violence and the escalation of violence which may follow from a relatively minor incident such as an arrest for drunken driving. Empirical studies (see McPhail and Miller, 1973) have shown that large assemblies can be quickly formed in urban ghettos and on college campuses by virtue of the immediate access of large numbers of people in the vicinity. Physical access is also facilitated by major pedestrian and vehicle intersections in the heart of densely populated residential areas and a majority of the 1967 riots in the United States started in or near such areas. It was also found that the majority of these riots originated during the evening or at weekends when large numbers of people were available. It is the 'long hot summers' when everyone is out on the streets at night which may spark off disturbances.

How do people know that something is going on? It is often alleged that news of disturbances or riots on radio or television mobilizes people to come to the area and that later disturbances ('copy-cat' rioting) in other areas are triggered off by such reports. The Kerner Commission (Kerner *et al.*, 1968) in the United States which had been explicitly asked to investigate the role of the mass media in riots found very little evidence in support of this view. Scarman (1982), however, came to the conclusion that the media bore responsibility for the escalation of the disorders (including the looting) in Brixton. Very often, however, it is found that news of rioting travels by word of mouth. Indeed, if riots were caused by information from the mass media, how would one explain their spread in the past? As Field (1982, p. 26) put it, 'when social controls break down, the spread of disorder is dictated by the available means of communication' and he cites Rudé (1967) who points out that eighteenth-century food riots spread through France primarily along river valleys. Southgate (1982) in investigating the disturbances in 1981 in Handsworth, Birmingham, found that of those who were actively involved seventy-five per cent said they knew *in advance*. Their responses 'emphasize very strongly the importance of rumour, gossip and the development of an atmosphere of expectation' (Southgate, 1982, p. 25).

critical mass Sullivan (1977) and also Lang and Lang (1968) proposed that a 'critical mass' of people is required to spark off a riot. They do not undervalue the importance of precipitating events, for instance some contact between members of the black community and the police as when police raid a club frequented by blacks (this sparked off a riot in Detroit in 1967, and in 1980 the raid by police on a café in the St. Paul's area of Bristol led to a riot there). Nevertheless they hold that it is not the grievances people have but the size of a crowd which matters in a riot since 'the larger the crowd, the more easily it can sustain the communication and indications of attitudes and emotions that will influence the behaviour of individuals in the crowd' (Sullivan, 1977, p. 52). Lang and Lang (1968) suggest that a 'critical mass' is enough people ready to go into action against control agents, though 'enough' is not further defined. Not all the people on the streets participate in disturbances, however: Southgate (1982) found that only four per cent of his sample of local residents aged sixteen to thirty-four reported active involvement in rioting but twenty per cent had been on the streets at some time during the troubles (and that figure rose to twenty-five per cent for those aged between sixteen and nineteen). However, it is likely that his interviewees may, for very obvious reasons, have under-reported their own involvement.

4.4   The causes of riots

Crowd phenomena are not explicable in terms of social psychological principles alone though the work briefly reviewed here throws some light on the psychological processes at work in the crowd. To fully understand riots and similar outbursts one must investigate the underlying longer-term problems of the areas where rioting occurs, as well as the nature of contemporary events which trigger off particular disturbances.

relative deprivation

There is some contemporary as well as historical evidence that riots occur in conditions of relative deprivation, that is, when people feel deprived in comparison to others in their society. Thus, riots in the United States occurred in the 1960s mainly in black ghetto areas in which young men grew increasingly frustrated at the extent of unemployment and the social conditions in which they lived compared with the greater affluence amongst other people in their country. American research (McPhail, 1971) showed that the poorest were less likely to riot than more affluent groups (since the latter may, in fact, be more frustrated at their relative lack of opportunity and status than the former). In Britain in 1981 white, black and Asian youngsters rioted, probably because their expectations of work, training and prospects were not fulfilled in inner-city conditions. Unemployment was by far the most common reason given for the disturbances in the locality studied by Southgate (1982) though American studies showed that whilst riots occurred in areas of high unemployment both rioters and non-rioters were equally likely to be unemployed. As Field (1982, p. 11) says: 'It therefore remains possible that unemployment was a causal factor in the riots, although it would achieve its effect through a sense of grievance communicated to the whole ghetto community, rather than through individual unemployed persons becoming more likely to riot'.

If, against the background of deep frustration, one looks at immediate trigger points, one is struck by how frequently both American studies of the 1960s and current British studies show that riots are triggered off by resentment with police action ('over-policing'). Recognizing that the immediate trigger may be police activity does not put all the blame on the police but it does imply that the police are not wholly blameless irrespective of the fact that the main cause of riots may be existing frustration (of the young or the black, for instance). Unfortunately what seems to be the case is that law enforcement by the police is looked upon with suspicion in areas of tension and frustration. Furthermore, the police are easily identified targets and they are for rioters both the symbol and reality of the authority of the society which has frustrated them in the first place. It is therefore important for the police to establish good relations with all groups in society (Scarman, 1982). But, even more so, we need to learn to understand and to tackle the historic and contemporary roots of the dissatisfaction which erupts into riots – whether such dissatisfactions are due to religious, racial or economic discrimination and inequality. Riots also denote political frustration and a sense that the ordinary political remedies are not available to the rioters. Violent actions by crowds may bring in their wake reassessments and social changes and initiatives including possibly also the creation of new social movements (the subject matter of the next Unit). If such rethinking follows on from riots, their effects may prove not to be wholly destructive.

4.5 Conclusions to section 4

After working through this section and the reading associated with it, you may well feel that you do not fully understand crowd phenomena. This would not be your fault since the research I discussed addresses only segments of the overall phenomenon. Crowd behaviour, however, is a live and topical issue and that is why I have included this section even though no wholly satisfactory explanations of crowd phenomena can be provided. Both the public and social scientists are interested in the apparently strange and indeed frightening behaviour in which individuals engage in a crowd. Very often 'crowds' are, therefore, treated as something very different from 'groups' and yet if you think back to the experiments by Milgram (1974) and Zimbardo (1973), you will have instances of dramatic and frightening behaviour of people in *groups* (rather than *crowds*). These group members, too, are behaving in ways which are uncharacteristic of them as individuals. I have, therefore, tried to relate the concepts used in crowd research to the analysis of group phenomena.

One other point; social psychologists have taken the crowd into the laboratory by manipulating such hypothesized characteristics as anonymity or deindividuation. We have seen that they were not wholly successful in doing this. But, even if they had been, do you think such research captures the flavour of crowd phenomena? Can we indeed generalize from laboratory findings to the wider world (even given that events in the 'wider world' have provided the raw input into the laboratory situation)? You have had many examples in this Block of real-life events – for instance, conformity, leadership or bystander apathy – being taken into the laboratory and studied under controlled conditions. Equally, new ideas and concepts arising from such research have been taken out of the laboratory and their appropriateness or validity tested in real life. This approach is exemplified in Reicher's study of the events in St. Paul's in Bristol in 1980.

5   CONCLUSIONS

5.1   Do we now know what is meant by a group?

Throughout this Block a variety of definitions for groups have been given and I have avoided the difficult and possibly fruitless attempt to provide *one* definition by referring to groups as an *area of study* (in the conclusions to section 1). There are three reasons why it is so difficult to provide one overall and agreed definition of groups.

(a)   A simple definition will not embrace all the subleties we have come across in this Block. For instance, a group can be defined as a collection of individuals who see themselves and/or are seen by others as members of a group. Such a definition is, at the most, a starting-point.

(b)   The concept of group may encompass anything from small face-to-face groups to large groups such as a nation.

(c)   Some of the words used in talking about groups, since they denote a psychological relationship or cognitive process or both, can be used about a variety of groups. For instance, a small face-to-face group such as a gang of children can be referred to as a primary group, as a membership group and, if the children treat it as such for certain aspects of their lives, as a reference group. If the street around the corner has produced another gang, the children in each group are likely to think of their own gang as an ingroup and of the other gang as an outgroup.

However, apart from the concepts 'primary' and 'face-to-face' which by definition only refer to small groups, all these descriptive or explanatory labels can also be used about large groups such as neighbourhood groups or racial, religious or national groups.

One important thing to understand about groups is that at all times we have multiple group memberships. We can at one and the same time be members of a family, a work group, a study group, a religious group, an ethnic group, a fan club, a sports club, of Yorkshire and England and so on and these group memberships need not be mutually exclusive, though I am not suggesting that they are free of tension. Again, several implications of this multiple group membership need to be noted. First, not all these group memberships are equally salient (that is, psychologically important) to a person at a given time or in given circumstances. Secondly, some of my examples refer to small groups, others belong to the societal level of analysis, but all can be referred to as groups – ingroups or outgroups, membership or reference groups.

You may recall that in the Block introduction I stressed the importance of being clear about the level of analysis at which one is operating – the individual, the group or society. It is, in fact, as we have seen throughout our discussions in this Block, not always easy to do this, again for several reasons. Thus, as my example of multiple group memberships has indicated, some groups are, psychologically speaking, groups (in that members relate to each other and membership has effects on the members) but they are at the same time societal level concepts such as nations, ethnic groups, the handicapped, the middle class, old-age pensioners and so on. Furthermore, whilst it is logical and analytically convenient to refer to different levels of analysis, in practice these levels intrude into each other. Thus, how you relate to others, say, in a work group, may be influenced by your other group memberships: for instance, in Northern Ireland to be a Catholic may affect relationships with Protestant workmates; in England, whilst religion may not be an issue, race sometimes is.

Throughout this Block we have had many examples of the intrusion of both the individual and the societal levels into the group level of analysis. To recall just two examples: Asch (section 1.5) who focused on group pressure found great *individual* differences in the reactions of his subjects and later experiments using his paradigm showed the influence of *societal* norms, that is, in certain historical periods and in different countries more or less conformity was in evidence; Wetherall, in studying the formation and behaviour of 'minimal' groups (section 3.5), found that Maori children differed from their European counterparts in their societal norms of generosity to outsiders and hence behaved differently from the European children in the same experimental situation. This is, of course, what one should expect unless one mistakenly thought that face-to-face group membership obliterates everything else – individual differences as much as cultural differences. One lesson to be learnt, therefore, concerns the extent to which we can generalize from experiments carried out in one culture to people in general.

Whilst we may not be able to conclude this Block by providing one all-inclusive definition for groups, we can be reasonably precise about the nature and psychological implications of the various kinds of groups we have studied and the nature of the influence processes at work among members or between members of different groups.

There is, of course, not complete agreement on all points. Thus, for instance, we have seen that how minorities and majorities within a group affect each other (section 1.6) has not been finally resolved. In general, however, there has been a move from looking on groups as arising from and meeting certain psychological needs to looking on groups as a number of people who perceive and identify themselves as members of the same social category. But these later developments (which reflect the general movement of psychology and social psychology towards cognitive theories) do not discredit earlier ones. If you are asked why people form groups you can validly reply that (on occasions) they do so because they need each other (to complete a task or for mutual emotional support) *or* you can – equally correctly – reply that (on occasions) they see themselves as a group because they share the same social identity. One reason why these different types of explanation neither contradict each other nor are mutually exclusive may be because they refer to different *stages* in the formation and existence of groups. Thus, as Turner (1982) himself agrees, the creation of a social identity (which he sees as the prerequisite for group formation) may depend on such variables as similarity, proximity, the perception of a common fate or shared threat. These are the same variables that earlier theorists, held to be important for the formation and cohesion of groups. Hence, the view that some groups are formed because members have the opportunity to meet or have, initially, some common need, interest or goal, or share personal characteristics, and so on, is not invalidated by the view that 'a social group can be usefully conceptualized as a number of individuals who have internalized the same social category membership as a component of their self-concept' (Turner, 1982, p. 36). The latter may follow on the former though one can be a member of a group without necessarily identifying to that extent with it.

Sometimes differences are mainly semantic. Thus when Cooley pointed out, at the beginning of this century, that small primary groups are 'natural' and that they, rather than the individual, form the basic human entity he was not so far removed from Tajfel and his colleagues when they showed in recent years in their experiments on 'minimal groups' that groups are formed quite spontaneously so that their members can set their own group off against outsiders. The terminology of their explanations may differ but they describe the same phenomenon.

Quite apart from the problem of defining groups, I raised the question in the Block introduction of whether we need the concept of group at all or whether the phenomena normally considered when groups are studied can be explained in other terms. I think this Block has shown that group theorists focus on issues and questions which are ignored by other social psychologists. Furthermore, the concept of group is required to refer to those interactions which are not wholly explicable in terms of interpersonal relations. Indeed much of this Block has been concerned with demonstrating that group membership is important to the individual and virtually universal.

Some unpalatable aspects are linked with the phenomenon of the group. Group membership, as we have seen, can be used to deliberately influence the individual (and this was the subject matter of section 2); and, in order to experience the satisfaction of group membership, people almost always treat other groups or individuals as outgroups (the subject matter of section 3).

5.2 Some paradoxes and unanswered questions

The boundaries between the individual and the group are difficult to chart and may remain *paradoxical*, because, as we have seen in this Block as well as throughout the course, the individual is a constructor as well as a reactor, free but constrained, unique but influenced by present and past circumstances. Thus, one may ask how far social identity defines personal identity? I have described (in section 3) that a social identity may be thrust on people (because they are seen by outsiders as belonging to a particular category). How do people evaluate themselves when they know that they belong to a low status group? Does such perceived membership affect their self-esteem? Or can they mobilize ego-defence mechanisms to shield themselves against such judgements? And do they do so in terms of saying 'this may apply to others in this group but not to me' or do they repudiate the views of the outgroup as they apply not just to themselves but to all members of their group? That, presumably, depends on how much they value the particular group membership (even though, as I pointed out it may, initially, have been thrust on them). There is also the possibility that people generally prefer to think of themselves as individuals with unique characteristics (*unless* they are in a situation where group membership is salient and paramount) but are quite willing to describe others in terms of social categories.

The notion of ingroup and outgroup also gives rise to some unanswered questions. We have seen (in section 3) that people can look on each other as ingroup members in certain settings but not in others, for instance when working down a mine white workers may feel a sense of solidarity with black fellow-workers but this may not remain so above ground. I have also shown that the mere presence of people, for instance bystanders at the scene of an emergency where a person needs help, does not of itself lead to the inclusion of the victim in the bystanders' ingroup (as evidenced by the extent to which help is or is not offered) though one might have expected this on the basis of Tafjel's work on 'minimal groups'. Indeed, there is the extraordinary phenomenon of the American nation treating its own Vietnam veterans as outcasts. It has been repeatedly reported that the soldiers (who were almost all national service conscripts rather than volunteers and hence no different from their compatriots) were vilified and refused jobs on their return and their unemployment rate, ten years after the ending of the war, is still higher than that of comparable groups. Whilst one can readily appreciate that Americans are ashamed of the defeat they suffered (militarily and in their political objectives) it is still extraordinary that, in order to vent these feelings, they turn their own soldiers into an outgroup and do not extend to them sufficient help to overcome the horrors of war they experienced.

Finally, I want to take up three further issues which are relevant to the study of groups. The first concerns ethics, the second validity, the third strategies for change.

5.3 The ethics of research and of the implementation of research

As I am writing, a movement for 'animal liberation' is gaining adherents and publicity in Britain. The members of this movement not only object to the extent to which animals are used in medical and cosmetic research laboratories and the painful and often fatal procedures which are used on them but they wish to establish that animals should be treated with dignity as of right and not be used in laboratories at all. My purpose is not to argue for or against this position but to point out that no such movement exists to protect human subjects in laboratory experiments. As we have seen, for instance in Milgram's experiments on obedience to authority (section 1.4) or in Zimbardo's experimental prison (section 2.3.6), human participants in experiments, whilst not subjected to physical pain, are exposed to situations which they will find disturbing during and after the event. Of course, I am not the first person to point this out and a great deal of heart-searching has taken place among psychologists. Several points tend to be advanced in justification of such experimental research.

First, that through, for instance, simulating conditions of captivity we can learn how not to break down in such conditions or we can even ameliorate life in prisons. That is true but, as I pointed out, the evidence and insights from such studies have also been used to refine interrogation techniques.

Secondly, the problems exist before the psychologist turns to studying them or to advocate solutions for them. Thus, captivity, authoritarian pressures, or for that matter selection for education or employment are all facts of contemporary life. If, for instance, psychologists develop or refine batteries of tests for selection, they may claim to be merely technicians who devise the means for pre-existing ends. The psychologist is part of society, not outside it. If, later on, such tests can be shown to have discriminated against members of certain social classes or ethnic groups or that, indeed, they are invalid, the psychologists can claim not to have foreseen such developments. Researching intelligence or intelligence testing is, at a given time, not seen as unethical. But, as I have stated before, whenever change-agents (which would include psychologists devising tests or advocating the acceptance of technological changes) set out to bring about changes in people or the physical or social environment, they need not only to question their own motives but also to think ahead to the likely undesirable (as well as the desirable) outcomes of their actions in the short or long run. A good example here might be a social psychologist advising a third world country on how to introduce birth control measures and assure their take-up by the target population. Will such measures affect family structure and relationships? Will the advocated measures, in fact, fail precisely because these matters have not been considered?

Thirdly, given that psychologists carry out disturbing experiments (as technicians of society or, as they may think at the time, purely in the pursuit of new knowledge and insights) they maintain that they sensitively 'debrief' their subjects after such experiments (for instance, by telling them that the victim was not really given electric shocks) and hence manage to send them away happy rather than perturbed by the weakness or callousness of their own characters which they have revealed during the experiments. That seems a tall order, unlikely to be entirely successful and not an excuse for putting people into such potentially perturbing situations in the first place – even though there is some evidence (from a replication of Milgram's studies on obedience to authority which was carried out to evaluate variations in debriefing) to suggest that such procedures may help (Ring, Wallston and Corey, 1970).

Fourthly, psychologists may maintain that subjects have freely consented to participate in experiments. This in itself may not be true in that in many universities students have to put in a certain number of hours as subjects to be given 'credits' for their psychology courses (and this puts pressure on them to agree to participate). In any case, it is clearly impossible for a subject to give *informed* consent. Indeed, if they knew the true purpose of the experiment about to be participated in, it would defeat its objective and hence, as you have seen throughout this course, psychologists have had recourse to deception. One cannot say to subjects in advance of the event: 'We want to see under what precise conditions you will succumb to authoritarian pressure'. Informed consent is, of course, also a problem in testing new drugs because psychological expectations on the part of subjects as well as the experimenter may influence the outcome – hence the 'double-blind' procedures usually adopted in drug-testing, where neither the nurse or doctor administering the treatment nor the patient know whether the drugs given are real drugs or placebos.

Social psychological experiments, focusing as they do on relationships with others, face greater ethical problems than do most psychology experiments. Thus, I do not think any great ethical problems arise in, say, verbal conditioning experiments where a subject is induced to repeat certain words by reinforcement from the experimenter (who, for instance, may nod in response to certain utterances). In pointing to some of these ethical problems, I do not advocate abolishing laboratory experiments in social psychology given that they provide us with insights into causal connections between independent and dependent variables. I am suggesting, however, that more thought should be given to ethical issues. This may well lead to some experiments into complex and sensitive issues being abandoned before they are carried out and to a search for alternative avenues of research, particularly natural or field experiments. The latter, of course, also present ethical problems as is evidenced by the experiments I described (section 3.6) on bystander apathy which took place in a genuine subway carriage with genuine travellers as subjects. They, too, may have been uneasy after the event about their attitudes or behaviour towards the (apparently) sick or handicapped person who had a fall during the journey.

In other parts of the course we have discussed a range of methods and we have pointed out their advantages and disadvantages as tools of research and the extent to which ethical problems are associated with them. Here I was concerned to raise some ethical issues which directly refer to research described in this Block and to point to the problems associated in both carrying out the experiments and the possible misuse of their findings. However, in voicing these criticisms and worries about some of the *experiments* featured in this Block, we should not forget that ethical issues are important in *all* research – observation, interviews or psychometric tests may be intrusive and disturbing, too. We should also not forget, as has been mentioned several times, that it is experiments like those carried out by Asch, Milgram and Zimbardo which demonstrate the importance of the *situational* context in determining our actions. Hence such experiments form a very important counterpoint to research and theorizing which look for the roots of behaviour in the developmental history and acquired dispositions of individuals (such as the work on the authoritarian personality featured in Block 5).

5.4   Validity of research

Validity of research is also discussed in other Blocks and in the Metablock and hence here I merely want to reinforce this discussion insofar as it concerns the material in this Block.

A good deal of the evidence presented in this Block derives from laboratory experiments. You may think that some of the experiments presented here (or which you have studied earlier in the course or in other psychology courses) are artificial and remote from 'real' life. This issue is often discussed in terms of the **internal validity** 'internal' and 'external' validity of experiments. Briefly, internal validity refers to the conclusions that can be properly derived from a particular experiment which has set out to test a particular hypothesis. External validity refers to the **external validity** generalizability of experimental findings to other setting or populations. This is nowadays sometimes referred to as 'ecological validity'. Many experiments have **ecological validity** been criticized as lacking such ecological validity for a variety of reasons. Most usually, it is asserted that the experiment is artificial and does not resemble real life and that the subjects are drawn from restricted samples of the population (frequently only from students). With regards to experiments in groups these criticisms can be contained (if not wholly rebutted) in a number of ways.

First of all, as we have seen, most of the experiments I have described derive from real-life concerns – be they conformity, obedience to authority, minority and majority influence in the group, indoctrination, bystander apathy, intergroup relations and so on. What the social psychologists concerned with one or other of these issues have done is to take a real-life problem, generate hypotheses about the causal connections between various variables and test these in controlled conditions. Where there is artificiality, it is likely to come about by the *isolation* of these variables in the laboratory, whilst in real life they may occur in combination with others. This focus on selected variables is, however, also the strength of laboratory experiments. After careful laboratory research, as we have seen for instance in the work on bystander apathy and on conflict between groups, the preliminary laboratory findings can be further tested in field experiments or they can be compared to data gained from observation in real life or from interviews or surveys. One example of this flow from the laboratory to real life is Reicher's study of an actual riot which was carried out in order to test the appropriateness of a theoretical concept derived mostly from laboratory work. The use of such a variety of methods may well result, eventually, in ecologically valid findings and insights. Hence we need not worry unduly whether one particular set of experiments has or has not external validity so long as it is not unjustifiably claimed that it has such validity and it is understood that these experiments form part of a wider-ranging research process. As I have pointed out, however, in the area of social psychology I have discussed here, we are still short of medium-range theories (that is, comprehensive theories which can encompass those theories which initially focused on only a limited range of situations, behaviours or experiences). Thus we have been unable to encompass all group phenomena in one unified theory and we need to accept, for the time being, the existence in social psychology of unconnected and often contradictory theories.

Another reason, of course, why experiments may not reaveal the 'whole' truth arises from the fact that subjects behave in experiments (as elsewhere) in terms of the *meanings* they attribute to the situation in which they find themselves. I have specifically mentioned this in section 1.6 in discussing which variables may lead to conformity to, and which to deviance from, the majority in experiments on conformity. The point, however, is more general. In the laboratory one may establish whether different kinds of subjects do or do not interpret the experimental situation in the same way. This can be deduced from the actual findings and, particularly, from post-experimental interviews. Perhaps you remember that quite early on in the Block I mentioned that Sherif's subjects in the experiments using the autokinetic effect were *not* aware that they had been influenced by others in arriving at their judgements and yet the experimental evidence clearly demonstrated such influence. To obtain from subjects their subjective views as to the meaning the situation has for them often helps the experimenter to refine her or his conclusions or to change some aspect in subsequent experiments such that subjects are more likely to interpret the experimental situation in a way that will reflect more appropriately the external reality (which the experimenter has taken in a simplified form into the laboratory). Post-experimental interviews (which reveal the meanings of a situation for the subjects) are, therefore, of use to the experimenter and have been quite generally adopted. However, we still would not know whether the subject would interpret a real-life situation in similar ways to the experimental situation which has been set up as an approximate analogue of some real life issue. Outside the laboratory many more factors influence the individual's perception of a situation and her or his role in it and hence her or his reactions. Once more I must emphasize that laboratory findings need to be followed up in the field and a variety of research methods needs to be employed to unravel successfully the complex factors governing people's perceptions and actions, whether alone or with others. *All* research methods have shortcomings and are limited in their capacity to produce valid findings and insights. In combination they may enable us to gain a better understanding of the phenomenon under investigation.

5.5 Strategies for change

In this Block we have followed two strands. One was concerned with developments in theory and methodology. The other focused on changes in the topics which have been investigated (for instance, a move from the study of conformity to that of innovation). These strands intertwined in that the new topics studied benefited from the increasing sophistication of social psychologists in their theoretical starting-points and their research tools. Thus, a focus on issues pushed to the forefront by the changing societal context does not preclude studying them in as 'purely' a scientific manner as possible, nor does the desire to be useful to society (which I have pointed out was characteristic of many early as well as some contemporary social psychologists) necessarily imply prejudgement or bias. Nevertheless the way issues are formulated or the variables selected for study may depend on one's values. I have also pointed to the problems associated with funding and other sponsorship. Furthermore, we are today more concerned (as psychologists and as citizens) with the autonomy of the individual, and the term 'social engineering', which Lewin (section 2.2) used approvingly, has now acquired a menacing and manipulative connotation. Thus there are ethical (as well as practical issues) involved, not only in studying social issues, but in implementing research findings.

We have, today, more knowledge (for instance concerning the implications of group membership for the individual) and such knowledge can be used to support a range of value positions. Thus, as we have seen throughout this Block, group membership can be rewarding and supportive to individuals or it can be used to influence their attitudes or behaviour in ways they would not have chosen freely and as individuals. The *same* knowledge, therefore, can be used to prepare individuals to resist undue pressures or to apply such pressures to them. In the Course Reader (Murphy, John and Brown, 1984) we have pointed out, in connection with the 'desegregation debate', that at a given time we may realize as psychologists that we do not have enough knowledge to arrive at finite views, and yet as citizens we may wish to intervene to remedy what are seen as glaring injustices.

Given that ethical concerns should make us cautious in applying our knowledge, there are still other barriers to implementing social psychological findings. Put baldly, these arise from the fact that complex social phenomena which we might wish to influence – conformity, racism, authoritarianism, intergroup conflict and so on – rarely have *psychological* solutions. Thus, in order to change people's attitudes and behaviour we may need to change the societal context. I have already referred to this in the conclusions to section 3 where I pointed out that to change racial prejudice one needs to implement legal and economic changes so that the context is provided in which better relations can develop or can be fostered.

Let us look at some examples. If you wish to help smokers to reduce their smoking, farmers to adopt new methods of cultivation or fathers to be more involved in the upbringing of their children, then, I would suggest, you need to consider your strategy as it applies to the individual, the group *and* the societal context.

Why do people smoke? Some may have an oral fixation in Freudian terms and may be thought to require individual psychoanalytic treatment. Others may have simply formed a habit which they find difficult to break. They may, initially, have started smoking not because it simulated the pleasures of the breast or bottle but because it made them feel adult or 'macho' and was the norm in their social surroundings. Such people and indeed those who smoke for 'deep-seated' reasons may not need psychoanalysis but may respond to behaviour therapy and/or group psychotherapy at a smoking clinic. *But* whichever therapy may have helped them initially, to sustain their newly learned non-smoking behaviour they are likely to need continued support from a special group or from their families or workmates. Furthermore, changes in their wider surroundings should also be effected so that their individual endeavours are helped by the prohibition of smoking in public places such as offices, libraries and trains. Such prohibitions give a seal of approval to the individual's own struggles and reduce the opportunities of reverting to the old habit of smoking.

Consider the farmers. Many studies in developing societies have shown that farmers are quick to learn new methods but slow to implement them. Implementation does not only depend on learning new skills (the individual level) and the approval of others in a similar situation (the group level), it usually also requires social system changes – the building of a road from the village to the nearest market town (so that the increased produce can be marketed), the setting-up of a cooperative bank (so that farmers need not sell their crop immediately but can negotiate a good price) and so on.

What about our third example, the involvement of fathers in the upbringing of their children? At first sight this seems an entirely personal matter (the individual level) and yet, of course, the father's attitudes and expectations mesh (or need to mesh) with those of his wife and with those of their friends (the group level). Wives and mothers have increasingly moved from their traditional home-bound role into the wider world of work (even when there is no pressing financial need for this). This changed lifestyle has enabled (though some might say forced) fathers to adopt an increasing involvement with their children. 'Society' will need to respond to this new situation by furthering it (through taxation changes, statutory rights to paternity leave, and so on) or by hindering it (by different taxation changes and increased support to mothers who do not take employment outside their homes).

If, then, you are interested in applying social psychological knowledge you need to think out at what level (the personal, group or societal) intervention would be most effective, most beneficial and least harmful. You might well end up by joining a pressure group or social movement (the topic of the next Unit) to advocate social system changes rather than using your energies to help people directly on a psychological level.

Notes

1 Many experimenters have used the terms public change and private change as interchangeable with manifest change and latent change. Strictly speaking, public and private should refer to the extent an individual is prepared for others to be aware of her or his position, that is, we are concerned with what I previously termed 'mode of response'. Manifest and latent change, on the other hand, refer to the extent an individual accepts an advocated position and the presumed permanency of the effect, latent refering to the more deep-seated and therefore more important and long-term effect (internalization).

Public and private responses arise from *interpersonal* aspects (such as perceived social pressure); manifest and latent refer to *intrapersonal* aspects (the extent to which the individual has altered her or his cognitions).

There are also some differences in the way the words, 'minority' and 'majority' are used. Sometimes 'minority' is used to denote the advocacy of a view which is deviant to general beliefs about, say, the causes of pollution or unemployment. Sometimes 'minority' refers to the *number* of people who stand out against the majority (usually instructed by the experimenter to adopt a certain position) as in the Asch paradigm or in Moscovici's experiments concerning the naming of slides which are objectively blue. The word minority tends nowadays to be used also to refer to those whose position in society is weak – be they women (though numerically in a majority) or blacks (also in the majority in South Africa and in many of the states in the United States) or members of a persecuted and economically weak religious group, whether numerically in the minority or not.

2 After the Korean War, the Americans defined *indoctrination* as an effort to change a person's viewpoint while she or he is still a thinking individual by regulating her or his thoughts and actions (Kinkead, 1959, p. 31).

3 Weber (1921) coined the phrase 'charismatic leader' (from the Greek 'charisma' which means divinely inspired power) for those leaders who attract a following because of their strong personalities. Weber points out that charismatic leaders tend to emerge when there is a crisis or a state of distress and uncertainty. Such a leader may, in Freudian terms, represent a common ego-ideal for the group (Freud, 1956).

4 The Japanese consider *hara-kiri* (suicide) to be the ultimate expression of autonomy, in contrast to Christian religions which condemn suicide (as throwing away God's gift of life). In Britain, in addition to religious disapproval, suicide was a criminal offence until the 1950s, that is, people who attempted but failed to commit suicide could be, and frequently were, charged with a criminal offence.

5 This paragraph was written before the outbreak of hostilities between Britain and the Argentine in 1982. It reflects my experience in World War Two. These more recent events, however, precisely underscore these words.

6 You have earlier (section 1.6) come across Latané's 'social impact theory' which states that all participants in a group are sources of influence. This view is a generalization from Latané and Darley's findings that bystanders to an emergency are less likely to intervene if others are present than if they are alone. If others are present, the responsibility for intervention is psychologically diffused. Social impact theory suggests that this process is more general and can lead to a diffusion or division of other social forces.

Further reading

If, at some time, you would like to get more deeply involved in some of the issues discussed in this Block, I would advise you to go, in the first instance, to the sources (books as well as journals) mentioned in the text for the area of your interest. Such reading will, of course, provide you with further ideas and references. Since many of you may not have access to specialist libraries, I would like to mention again here some books, already referred to in the text, which should be widely available and which I have found very stimulating. Inevitably such a brief list is eclectic and may not correspond to your own interests.

R. J. LIFTON (1961) *Thought Reform and the Psychology of Totalism: A Study of 'Brainwashing' in China*, London, Gollancz.
This book discusses the techniques employed in 'brainwashing' and presents five fascinating case histories.

S. MILGRAM (1974) *Obedience to Authority*, London, Tavistock.
This book is of general interest as it discusses an important contemporary issue. It also demonstrates how a psychologist works as he moves from his original experiment to test a range of hypotheses. (One chapter is reprinted in the Course Reader, Murphy, John and Brown, 1984.)

S. NAIPAUL (1981) *Black and White*, London, Sphere.
This book traces the ideas generated in California in the 1960s and 1970s in the white radical and Black Power movements and analyses the events culminating in the mass suicide of the followers of the Reverend Jim Jones against this wider context. A chilling (but fascinating) account which is definitely not bedside reading.

H. TAJFEL (ed.) (1982) *Social Identity and Intergroup Relations*, London, Cambridge University Press.
This book brings together the work of different researchers, several of whom have been mentioned in the Block. Again, the topic area of the book is of contemporary importance and it focuses on many aspects of 'groups'.

P. WATSON (1980) *War on the Mind: The Military Uses and Abuses of Psychology*, Harmondsworth, Penguin Books.
The title is self-explanatory and the book echoes some of the anxieties I expressed in the Block concerning sponsorship or abuse of knowledge.

References

ADORNO, T., FRENKEL-BRUNSWICK, E., LEVINSON, D. and SANFORD, N. (1950) *The Authoritarian Personality*, New York, Harper and Row.

ALLEN, V. L. (1975) 'Social support for nonconformity', in Berkowitz, L. (ed.) *Advances in Experimental Social Psychology*, Vol. 8, New York, Academic Press.

ALLPORT, G. W. (1954) *The Nature of Prejudice*, Cambridge, Mass., Addison-Wesley.

AMIR, Y. (1969) 'Contact hypothesis in ethnic relations', *Psychological Bulletin*, Vol. 71, pp. 319–42.

ASCH, S. E. (1952) 'Effects of group pressure upon modification and distortion of judgements', in Swanson, G. E., Newcomb, T. M. and Hartley, E. L. (eds) *Readings in Social Psychology*, New York, Holt, Rinehart and Winston.

ASCH, S. E. (1955) 'Opinions and social pressures', *Scientific American*, Vol. 193, November, pp. 31–55.

BARTON, W. *et al.* (1974) *Social Psychology: Explorations in Understanding*, Del Mar, Cal., CRM Books.

BERGER, P. L. and LUCKMAN, T. (1967) *The Social Construction of Reality*, London, Allen Lane.

BERKOWITZ, L. (1956) 'Personality and group position', *Sociometry*, Vol. 19, pp. 210–22.

BETTELHEIM, B. (1961) *The Informed Heart*, London, Thames and Hudson.

BILLIG, M. and TAJFEL, H. (1973) 'Similarity and categorization in intergroup behaviour', *European Journal of Social Psychology*, Vol. 3, No. 1, pp. 27–53.

BION, W. R. (1961) *Experiences in Groups*, London, Macmillan.

BRAY, R. M. *et al.* (1982) 'Social influence by group members with minority opinions: a comparison of Hollander and Moscovici', *Journal of Personality and Social Psychology*, Vol. 43, No. 1, pp. 78–88.

BROWN, R. J. and TURNER, J. C. (1981) 'Interpersonal and intergroup behaviour', in Turner, J. C. and Giles, H. (eds) (1981) *Intergroup Behaviour*, Oxford, Blackwell.

BYRNE, D. (1971) *The Attraction Paradigm*, New York, Academic Press.

CARTWRIGHT, D. (1979) 'Contemporary social psychology in historical perspective', *Social Psychology Quarterly*, Vol. 42, No. 1, pp. 82–93.

COCH, L. and FRENCH, J. R. P. (1948) 'Overcoming resistance to change, *Human Relations*, Vol. 1, pp. 512–32.

COOLEY, C. H. (1902) *Human Nature and the Social Order* (New York, Shocken, 1964).

COSER, L. A. (1967) *Continuities in the Study of Social Conflict*, New York, Free Press.

DAVIS, J. H. (1969) *Group Performance*, Reading, Mass., Addison-Wesley.

DAVIS, J. H. and HORNSETH, J. P. (1967) 'Discussion patterns and world problems', *Sociometry*, Vol. 30, pp. 91–103.

DEUTSCH, M. and COLLINS, M. E. (1951) *Interracial Housing: a Psychological Evaluation of a Social Experiment*, Minneapolis, University of Minnesota Press.

DIENER, E. (1980) 'Deindividuation: the absence of self-awareness and self-regulation in group members', in Paulus, P. B. (ed.) *Psychology of Group Influence*, Hillsdale, New Jersey, Erlbaum.

DURKHEIM, E. (1897) *Rules of Sociological Method* (New York, Free Press, 1950).

DWYER, P. M. (1979) 'An enquiry into the psychological dimensions of cult suicide', *Suicide and Life-threatening Behaviour*, Vol. 9, No. 2, pp. 120–7.

EHRENREICH, B. and ENLIGH, D. (1979) *For Her Own Good: 150 Years of the Experts' Advice to Women*, London, Pluto Press; an extract is reprinted in Murphy, J., John, M., and Brown, H. (1984) (Course Reader.)

ELLUL, J. (1965) *Propaganda: The Formation of Men's Attitudes*, New York, Vintage Books.

FESTINGER, L. (1953) *An Analysis of Compliant Behaviour*, in Sherif, M. and Wilson, M. O. (eds) (1953) *Group Relations at the Crossroads*, New York, Harper and Row.

FESTINGER, L. (1957) *A Theory of Cognitive Dissonance*, Evanston, Ill., Row, Peterson.

FESTINGER, L., PEPITONE, A. and NEWCOMB, T. (1952) 'Some consequences of deindividuation in a group', *Journal of Abnormal and Social Psychology*, Vol. 47, pp. 382–9.

FIEDLER, F. E. (1965) 'Engineer the job to fit the manager', *Harvard Business Review*, pp. 115–22.

FIEDLER, F. E. (1967) *A Theory of Leadership Effectiveness*, New York, McGraw-Hill.

FIEDLER, F. E. (1968) 'Personality and situational determinants of leadership effectiveness', in Cartwright, D. and Zander, A. (eds) *Group Dynamics*, New York, Harper and Row.

FIEDLER, F. E. (1971) 'Validation and extension of the contingency model of leadership effectiveness: a review of empirical findings', *Psychological Bulletin*, Vol. 76, pp. 128–48.

FIEDLER, F. E. (1972) 'Personality motivational systems and the behaviour of high and low LPC', *Human Relations* Vol. 25, pp. 391–412.

FIELD, S. (1982) 'Urban disorders in Britain and America: a review of research', in Field, S. and Southgate, P. (1982) *Public Disorder: A Home Office Research and Planning Unit Report*,, London, HMSO.

FRANKS, (LORD) (1983) *Falkland Islands Review*, Report of a Committee of Privy Councillors, CMND 8787, London, HMSO.

FREUD, S. (1921) *Group Psychology and the Analysis of the Ego* (Standard Edition, Vol. 18. London, Hogarth Press, 1955).

FROMM, E. (1941) *Escape from Freedom*, New York, Farrar and Rinehart (published as *Fear of Freedom*, London, Routledge and Kegan Paul).

GANS, H. J. (1972) *People and Plans: Essays on Urban Problems and Solutions*, Harmondsworth, Penguin Books.

GERARD, H. B. (1954) 'The anchorage of opinions in face-to-face groups', *Human Relations*, Vol. 7, pp. 313–26.

GOFFMAN, E. (1968) *Asylums*, Harmondsworth, Penguin Books.

GOFFMAN, E. (1971) *The Presentation of Self in Everyday Life*, Harmondsworth, Penguin Books.

GRAF, R. G. and RIDDELL, J. C. (1972) 'Helping behaviour as a function of interpersonal perception', *Journal of Social Psychology*, Vol. 86, pp. 227–31.

HARDY, K. R. (1957) 'Determinants of conformity and attitude change', *Journal of Abnormal and Social Psychology*, Vol. 54, pp. 289–94.

HEARST, CAMPBELL, P. (1983) *Every Secret Thing*, London, Arrow Books.

HEBB, D. O. *et al.* (1952) 'The effects of isolation upon attitudes, motivation and thought', *Fourth Symposium, Military Medicine I*, Defence Research Board, Canada.

HEWSON, D. (1982) 'Fireproof uniforms anger blacks', *The Times*, 22 April.

HOLLANDER, E. P. (1958) 'Conformity, status and idiosyncrasy credit', *Psychological Review*, Vol. 65, pp. 117–27.

HOLLANDER, E. P. and JULIAN, J. W. (1970) 'Studies in leader legitimacy, influence and innovation', in Berkowitz, L. (ed.) *Advances in Experimental Social Psychology*, Vol. 5, New York, Academic Press.

HOMANS, G. C. (1961) *Social Behaviour: Its Elementary Forms*, New York, Harcourt Brace Jovanovich.

HOVLAND, C. I. and JANIS, I. L. (1959) *Personality and Persuasibility*, New Haven, Yale University Press.

HOVLAND, C. I., JANIS, I. L. and KELLY, H. H. (1953) *Communication and Persuasion*, New Haven, Conn., Yale University Press.

HYMAN, H. H. (1942) *The Psychology of Status*, Archives of Psychology, No. 269, New York, Columbia University.

JAHODA, M. (1959) 'Conformity and independence – a psychological analysis', *Human Relations*, Vol. 12, pp. 99–120.

JAHODA, M. (1982) 'Individual and group', in Pines, M. and Rafaelsen, L. (eds) *The Individual and the Group, Vol. 1: Theory*, New York, Plenum Press.

JANIS, I. L. (1968) *Victims of group think: a psychological study of foreign policy decisions and fiascos*, Boston, Mass., Houghton Mifflin.

JENKINS, B. M. (1975) *Hostages and their Captors: Friends and Lovers* Santa Monica, California, Rand.

KELMAN, H. C. (1958) 'Compliance, Identification and Internalization: Three Processes of Attitude Change', *Journal of Conflict Resolution*, Vol. 2, pp. 51–60.

KERNER, O. *et al.* (1968) *Report of the National Advisory Commission on Civil Disorders*, Washington, DC, US Government Printing Office.

KINKEAD, E. (1959) *Why They Collaborated*, London, Longman.

LAING, R. D. (1970) *The Divided Self*, Harmondsworth, Penguin Books.

LANG, K. and LANG, G. E. (1968) 'Racial disturbances as collective protest', *American Behavioural Scientist*, Vol. 11, pp. 11–13.

LAPIERE, R. T. (1934) 'Attitudes versus actions', *Social Forces*, Vol. 13, pp. 230–7.

LARSEN, K. (1974) 'Conformity in the Asch experiment', *Journal of Social Psychology*, Vol. 94, pp. 303–4.

LARSEN, K. S. (1982) 'Cultural conditions and conformity: the Asch effect', *Bulletin of the British Psychological Society*, Vol. 35, p. 347.

LARSEN, K. S., TRIPLETT, J. S., BRANT, W. D. and LANGENBERG, D. (1979) 'Collaborator status, subject characteristics and conformity in the Asch paradigm', *Journal of Social Psychology*, Vol. 108, pp. 259–63.

LATANÉ, B. and DARLEY, J. M. (1968) 'Group inhibition of bystander intervention in emergencies', *Journal of Personality and Social Psychology*, Vol. 10, pp. 215–21.

LATANE, B. and RODIN, J. (1969) 'A lady in distress: inhibiting effects of friends and strangers on bystander intervention', *Journal of Experimental Social Psychology*, Vol. 5, pp. 189–202.

LATANÉ, B. and DARLEY, J. M. (1970) *The Unresponsive Bystander: Why Does He Not Help?*, New York, Appleton-Century-Crofts.

LATANÉ, B. and DARLEY, J. M. (1976) *Help in a Crisis: Bystander Response to an Emergency*, Morristown, New Jersey, General Learning Press.

LATANÉ, B. and NIDA, S. (1980) 'Social impact theory and group influence: a social engineering perspective', in Paulus, P. B. (ed.) *Psychology of Group Influence*, Hillsdale, New Jersey, Erlbaum.

LATANÉ, B. and WOLF, S. (1981) 'The social impact of majorities and minorities', *Psychological Review*, Vol. 88, No. 5, pp. 438–53.

LEAVITT, H. J. (1951) 'Some effects of certain communication patterns on group performance', *Journal of Abnormal and Social Psychology*, Vol. 46, pp. 38–50.

LE BON, G. (1895) *The Crowd: A Study of the Popular Mind* (London, Ernest Benn, 1952).

LEVY, L. (1960) 'Studies in conformity behaviour: a methodological note', *Journal of Psychology*, Vol. 50, pp. 39–41.

LEWIN, K. (1948) *Resolving Social Conflicts: Selected Papers on Group Dynamics*, New York, Harper and Brothers.

LEWIN, K., LIPPITT, R. and WHITE, R. (1939) 'Patterns of aggressive behaviour in experimentally created "social climates"', *Journal of Social Psychology*, Vol. 10, pp. 271–99.

LEWIN, K. (1947) 'Group decision and social change', in Newcomb, T. M. and Hartley, E. L. (eds) (1947) *Readings in Social Psychology*, New York, Holt, Rinehart and Winston.

LIFTON, R. J. (1957) 'Thought reform of Chinese intellectuals', *Journal of Social Issues*, Vol. 13, pp. 5–20.

LIFTON, R. J. (1961) *Thought Reform and the Psychology of Totalism: A Study of 'Brainwashing' in China*, London, Gollancz.

LUCHINS, A. S. and LUCHINS, E. H. (1955) 'On conformity with true and false communications', *Journal of Social Psychology*, Vol. 42, pp. 283–303.

McPHAIL, C., (1971) 'Civil disorder participation: a critical examination of recent research', *American Sociological Review*, Vol. 36, pp. 1058–71.

McPHAIL, C. and MILLER, D. (1973) 'The assembly process: a theoretical and empirical examination', *American Sociological Review*, Vol. 38, pp. 721–35.

MILGRAM, S. (1961) 'Nationality and conformity', *Scientific American*, Vol. 205, No. 6, pp. 45–51.

MILGRAM, S. (1974) *Obedience to Authority*, London, Tavistock. (Excerpt reprinted in Murphy, J., John, M. and Brown, H. (1984) (Course Reader); (set reading.)

MILGRAM, S. and TOCH, H. (1969) 'Collective behaviour: crowds and social movements', in Lindzey, G. and Aronson, E. (eds) (1969) *The Handbook of Social Psychology*, Vol. IV (2nd edn), Reading, Mass., Addison-Wesley.

MINARD, R. D. (1952) 'Race relationships in the Pocahontas coal fields', *Journal of Social Issues*, Vol. 25, pp. 29–44.

MINISTRY OF DEFENCE (1955) *Treatment of British Prisoners of War in Korea*, London, HMSO.

MOSCOVICI, S. (1980) 'Towards a theory of conversion behaviour', in Berkowitz, L. (ed.) *Advances in Experimental Social Psychology*, Vol. 13, New York, Academic Press.

MOSCOVICI, S. and FAUCHEUX, C. (1972) 'Social influence, conformity bias and the study of active minorities', in Berkowitz, L. (ed.) (1972) *Advances in Experimental Social Psychology*, Vol. 6, New York, Academic Press.

MOSCOVICI, S., LAGE, E. and NAFFRECHOUX, M. (1969) 'Influence of a consistant minority on the response of a majority in a color perception task', *Sociometry*, Vol. 32, pp.365–80.

MOSCOVICI, S. and NEMETH, C. (1974) 'Social influence II: minority influence', in Nemeth, C. (ed.) *Social Psychology: Classic and Contemporary Integrations*, Chicago, Rand McNally.

MUGNY G. (1982) *The Power of Minorities*, London, Acedemic Press.

MURPHY, J., JOHN, M. and BROWN, H. (eds.) (1984) *Dialogues and Debates in Social Psychology*, London, Lawrence Erlbaum (Course Reader).

NAIPAUL, S. (1981) *Black and White*, London, Sphere Books.

NEMETH, C. J. and WACHTLER, J. (1983) 'Creative problem solving as a result of majority versus minority influence', *European Journal of Social Psychology*, Vol. 13, pp. 45–55.

NEWCOMB, T. M. (1952) 'Attitude development as a function of reference groups: the Bennington study', in Swanson, G. E., Newcomb, T. M. and Hartley, E. L. (eds) *Readings in Social Psychology*, New York, Holt, Rinehart and Winston.

NEWCOMB, T. M. *et al.* (1967) *Persistence and Change: Bennington College and its Students after Twenty-five years*, New York, John Wiley and Sons.

NEWMAN, O. (1972) *Defensive Space*, New York, Macmillan.

ORNE, M. T. (1962) 'On the social psychology of the psychological experiment', *American Psychologist*, Vol. 17, No. 11, pp.776–83.

OSMOND, H. (1957) 'Function as the basis of psychiatric ward design', in Proshansky, H. M. *et al.* (1970) *Environmental Psychology: Man and his Physical Setting*, New York, Holt, Rinehart and Winston.

PELZ, E. B. (1958) 'Some factors in group decision', in Maccoby, E. E., Newcomb, T. M. and Hartley, E. L. (eds) (1958) *Readings in Social Psychology* (3rd edn), New York, Holt, Rinehart and Winston.

PERRIN, S. and SPENCER, C. (1981) 'Independence or conformity in the Asch experiment as a reflection of cultural and situational factors', *British Journal of Social Psychology*, Vol. 20, pp. 205–9.

PETTIGREW, T. F. (1958) 'Personality and socio-cultural factors in intergroup attitudes: a cross-national comparison', *Journal of Conflict Resolution*, Vol. 2, pp. 29–42.

PETTIGREW, T. F. (1964) *A Profile of the American Negro*, Princeton, Van Nostrand.

PETTIGREW, T. F. (1971) *Racially Separate or Together?* New York, McGraw-Hill.

PILIAVIN, I. M., RODIN, J. and PILIAVIN, J. (1969) 'Good samaritanism: an underground phenomenon?', *Journal of Personality and Social Psychology*, Vol. 13, pp. 289–99.

PILIAVIN, I. M., PILIAVIN, J. A. and RODIN, S. (1975) 'Costs, diffusion and the stigmatised victim', *Journal of Personality and Social Psychology*, Vol. 32, pp. 429–38.

PILIAVIN, J. A. and PILIAVIN, I. M. (1972) 'Effect of blood on reactions to a victim', *Journal of Personality and Social Psychology*, Vol. 23, pp. 353–62.

PILIAVIN, J. A. *et al.* (1981) *Emergency Intervention*, New York, Academic Press.

RAVEN, B. H. (1959) 'Social influence on opinions and the communication of related content', *Journal of Abnormal and Social Psychology*, Vol. 58, pp. 119–28.

REICHER, S. D. (1982) 'The determinants of collective behaviour', in Tajfel, H. (ed.) (1982) op cit.

REICHER, S. D. (1984) 'St. Paul's: a study in the limits of crowd behaviour', in Murphy, J., John, M. and Brown, H. (eds) (1984) (Course Reader). (Set reading.)

RING, K., WALLSTON, K. and COREY, M. (1970) 'Role of debriefing as a factor affecting subjective reaction to a Milgram type obedience experiment: an ethical enquiry', *Representative Research in Social Psychology*, Vol. 1, No. 1, pp. 67–88.

ROETHLISBERGER, F. J. and DICKSON, W. J. (1939) *Management and the Worker*, Cambridge, Mass., Harvard University Press.

ROKEACH, M. (1960) *The Open and Closed Mind*, New York, Basic Books.

ROKEACH, M. (1968) *Beliefs, Attitudes and Values*, San Francisco, Jossey-Bass.

ROSENTHAL, R. (1966) *Experimenter Effects in Behavioural Research*, New York, Appleton-Century-Crofts.

RUDÉ, G. (1967) *The Crowd in History*, New York, John Wiley and Sons.

SAVIN, H. B. (1973) 'Professors and psychological researchers: conflicting values in conflicting roles', *Cognition*, Vol. 2, No. 1, pp. 147–49. Reprinted in Murphy, J., John, M. and Brown, H. (eds) (1984) (Course Reader).

SAYLES, S. M. (1966) 'Supervisory style and productivity: review and theory', *Personnel Psychology*, Vol. 19, No. 3, pp. 275–86.

SCARMAN (The Right Honourable Lord Scarman) (1981) *The Brixton Disorders 10–12 April, 1981*, CMND 8427, London, HMSO. (Harmondsworth, Penguin Books, 1982.)

SCHACHTER, S. (1957) 'Duration, rejection and communication', *Journal of Abnormal and Social Psychology*, Vol. 46, pp. 190–207.

SCHEIN, E. H. (1956) 'The Chinese indoctrination program for prisoners of war', *Psychiatry*, Vol. 19, pp. 149–73.

SCHEIN, E. H. (1957) 'Reaction patterns to severe chronic stress in American Army prisoners of war', *Journal of Social Issues*, Vol. 13, pp. 21–30.

SCHWARTZ, S. H. and GOTTLIEB, A. (1976) 'Bystander reaction to a violent theft: crime in Jerusalem', *Journal of Personality and Social Psychology*, Vol. 34, pp. 1188–99.

SEALY, A. P. (1975) 'The jury: decision-making in a small group', in Brown, H. and Stevens, R. (eds) (1975) *Social Behaviour and Experience*, London, Hodder and Stoughton.

SHAW, M. E. (1971) *Group Dynamics: The Psychology of Small Group Behaviour*, New York, McGraw-Hill.

SHERIF, M. (1936) *The Psychology of Social Norms*, New York, Harper and Row.

SHERIF, M. and SHERIF, C. W. (1953) *Groups in Harmony and Tension*, New York, Harper Brothers.

SHERIF, M., WHITE, B. J. and HARVEY, O. J. (1955) *Experimental Study of Positive and Negative Intergroup Attitudes Between Experimentally Produced Groups: Robbers' Cave Study*, Norman, University of Oklahoma.

SHERIF, M., HARVEY, O. J., WHITE, B. J., HOOD, W. R. and SHERIF, C. (1961) *Intergroup Cooperation and Competition: The Robbers' Cave Experiment*, Norman, University of Oklahoma.

SHERIF, M. and SHERIF, C. (1969) *Social Psychology*, New York, Harper and Row.

SIEGEL, A. E. and SIEGEL, S. (1957) 'Reference groups, membership groups, and attitude change', *Journal of Abnormal and Social Psychology*, Vol. 55, pp. 360–4.

SIMPSON, M. A. (1976) 'Brought in dead', *Omega: Journal on Death and Dying*, Vol. 7, pp. 243–8.

SINGER, J. E., BRUSH, C. A. and LUBLIN, S. C. (1965) 'Some aspects of deindividuation: indentification and conformity', *Journal of Experimental Social Psychology*, Vol. 1, pp. 356–78.

SISTRUNK, F. and McDAVID, J. W. (1971) 'Sex variables in conformity behaviour', *Journal of Personality and Social Psychology*, Vol. 17, pp. 200–7.

SORRELL, W. E. (1978) 'Cults and cult suicide', *International Journal of Group Tensions*, Vol. 8, pp. 96–105.

SOUTHGATE, P. (1982) 'The disturbances of July 1981 in Handsworth, Birmingham: a survey of the views and experiences of male residents', in Field, S. and Southgate, P. (1982) *Public Disorder: A Home Office Research and Planning Unit Report*, London, HMSO.

STARK, M. J. A. *et al.*(1974) 'Some empirical patterns in a riot process', *American Sociological Review*, Vol. 39, pp. 865–76.

STEVENS, R. (1983) *Freud and Psychoanalysis*, Milton Keynes, Open University Press. (Set Book.)

SUDNOW, D. (1973) 'Dead on arrival', *Interaction*, November, pp. 23–31.

SULLIVAN, T. J. (1977) 'The "critical mass" in crowd behaviour: crowd size, contagion and the evolution of riots', *Humboldt Journal of Social Relations*, Vol. 4, No. 2, pp. 46–59.

TAJFEL, H. (1978) *Differentiation Between Social Groups: Studies in the Social Psychology of Intergroup Relations*, London, Academic Press.

TAJFEL, H. (ed.) (1982) *Social Identity and Intergroup Relations*, London/Paris, Cambridge University Press/Editions de la Maison des Sciences de l'Homme.

TAJFEL, H., BILLIG, M. G. and BUNDY, R. P. (1971) 'Social categorization and intergroup behaviour', *European Journal of Social Psychology*, Vol. 1, No. 2, pp. 149–78.

TAJFEL, H. and TURNER, J. (1979) 'An integrative theory of intergroup conflict', in Austin, G. W. and Worchel, S. (eds) (1979) *The Social Psychology of Intergroup Relations*, Monterey, California, Brooks/Cole.

TARDE, G. (1890) *The Laws of Imitation*, New York, Holt.

TRIST, E. L., HIGGINS, G. W., MURRAY, H. and POLLOCK, A. B. (1963) *Organisational Choice*, London, Tavistock.

TURNER, J. C. (1982) 'Towards a cognitive redefinition of the social group', in Tajfel, H. (ed.) (1982). op. cit.

WATSON, P. (1980) *War on the Mind: The Military Uses and Abuses of Psychology,* Harmondsworth, Penguin Books. (Excerpt reprinted in Murphy, J., John, M. and Brown, H. (1984) (Course Reader).

WEBER, M. (1921) *The Sociology of Charismatic Authority*, in Gerth, H. H. and Mills, C. W. (translaters and editors) *Max Weber: Essays in Sociology*, London, Oxford University Press.

WETHERALL, M. (1982) 'Cross-cultural studies of minimal groups: implications for the social identity theory of intergroup relations', in Tajfel, H. (ed.) (1982). op. cit.

WOHLSTETTER, R. (1962) *Pearl Harbour: Warning and Decision.* Stamford, Stamford University Press.

WOODWARD, J. (1965) *Industrial Organization: Theory and Practice*, London, Oxford University Press.

YEE, M. S. and LAYTON, T. N. (1981) *In My Father's House: The Story of the Layton Family and the Reverend Jim Jones*, New York, Holt, Rinehart and Winston.

ZIMBARDO, P. G. (1969) 'The human choice: individuation, reason and order versus deindividuation, impulse and chaos', in Arnold, W. J. and Levine, D. (eds) *Nebraska Symposium on Motivation*, Lincoln, University of Nebraska Press.

ZIMBARDO, P. G., BANKS, W. C., CRAIG, H. and JAFFE, D. (1973) 'A Pirandellian prison: the mind is a formidable jailer', *New York Times Magazine*, 8 April 1973, pp. 38–60.

ZIMBARDO, P. G. (1973) 'On the ethics of intervention in human psychological research with special reference to the "Stanford Prison experiment"', *Cognition*, Vol. 2, No. 2, pp. 243–55. Reprinted in Murphy, J., John, M. and Brown, H. (1984) (Course Reader).

Acknowledgements

Grateful acknowledgement is made to the following sources for material used in this unit:

Figures 1a and 1b from *An Outline in Social Psychology*, rev. edn. by Muzafer Sherif and Carolyn W. Sherif, copyright © 1948, 1956 by Harper and Row, Publishers, Inc., reprinted by permission of the publisher; *Figures 3a–d* copyright © 1965 by Stanley Milgram, from the film *Obedience*, distributed by New York University Film Library; *Figure 8* from J. Shirley 'Can those seige friendships last?' in *Sunday Times*, 25 November, 1979; *Figure 9* Professor Philip Zimbardo, Stanford University, California; *Figure 10* United Press International Inc.

Index of concepts